Investigating the Reasons University Students in the South Central United States Have to Retake First-Year English Composition

Investigating the Reasons University Students in the South Central United States Have to Retake First-Year English Composition

Edith Sue Kohner Burford

Mellen Studies in Education
Volume 98

The Edwin Mellen Press
Lewiston•Queenston•Lampeter

Library of Congress Cataloging-in-Publication Data

Burford, Edith Sue Kohner.
    Investigating the reasons university students in the South Central United States have to retake first-year English composition / Edith Sue Kohner Burford.
      p. cm. -- (Mellen studies in education ; v. 98)
    Includes bibliographical references and index.
    ISBN 0-7734-6314-3
    1. English language--Rhetoric--Study and teaching--Southern States. 2. Report writing--Study and teaching (Higher)--Southern States. 3. Basic writing (Remedial education)--Southern States. I. Title. II. Series.

PE1405.U6B87 2004
808'.042'0711075--dc22

2004052179

```
This is volume 98 in the continuing series
Mellen Studies in Education
Volume 98 ISBN 0-7734-6314-3
MSE Series ISBN 0-88946-935-0
```

A CIP catalog record for this book is available from the British Library

Copyright © 2004 Edith Sue Kohner Burford

All rights reserved. For information contact

        The Edwin Mellen Press   The Edwin Mellen Press
              Box 450   Box 67
          Lewiston, New York   Queenston, Ontario
          USA 14092-0450   CANADA L0S 1L0

                  The Edwin Mellen Press, Ltd.
                  Lampeter, Ceredigion, Wales
                UNITED KINGDOM SA48 8LT

            Printed in the United States of America

Dedication

I dedicate this book to my husband, Kenneth, who supported me throughout the entire process of researching and writing of this book.

Contents:

Preface by Gian S. Pagnucci, Ph.D	iii
Acknowledgments	ix

Chapter 1.   1
The Problem and Its Significance   1
    Introduction to History of the Area   1
    Problem   4

Chapter 2.   9
Review of the Literature   9
    Teaching Style   10
    Learning Style   12
    Cultural Identity   17
    Summary/Conclusion   30

Chapter 3.   33
Methodology: Data Collection   33
    Introduction   33
    Surveys   34
        Teaching Style   35
            Student Survey Questions   36
            Faculty Survey Questions   36
            Faculty Interview Questions   36
        Learning Style   37
            Student Survey Questions   37
            Faculty Survey Questions   37
            Faculty Interview Questions   38
        Cultural Identity   38
            Student Survey Questions   39
            Faculty Survey Questions   39
            Student Survey Additional Questions   40
    Interviews   40
    Teaching Styles   41
        Student Questions   41
        Faculty Questions   41
    Learning Styles   42
        Faculty Questions   42
    Interview Procedures   42
        Students   42
        Faculty   42

Chapter 4. 45
Analysis of the Data 45
    Student Surveys 45
    Analysis 46
    Faculty Surveys 60
    Student Interviews 73
        Interview Procedures 73
        Student Interviews 73
        Conclusion 80
    Faculty Interviews 80
        Interview Procedures 80
        Faculty Interviews 80

Chapter 5. 89
Discussion 89
    Student Discussion 89
    Faculty Discussion 92
    Conclusion 97
    For Further Study 99

Bibliography 103

Index 109

Appendices 111
    Appendix A: Memo to Instructors 112
    Appendix B: Student Informed Consent and Survey 114
    Appendix C: Faculty Informed Consent and Survey 120
    Appendix D: Student Informed Consent and Interview 124
    Appendix E: Faculty Informed Consent and Interview 128
    Appendix F: Map of Texas showing Counties 132

Preface

Race and Learning Style Conflicts in the Borderlands:
A Preface

By Gian S. Pagnucci, Ph.D.
Professor of English
Indiana University of Pennsylvania

> The block had many hues and many sounds, mainly black and brown hues and sounds, but others as well, yellows and olives, and variations on white [. . .] . I grew up among the poor, some passing through, some permanent residents. (Villanueva 16)

In his autobiography, *Bootstraps: From an American Academic of Color*, Victor Villanueva, Jr., talks about his struggle to find his place within the world of the academy, his work to carve out a place for himself. This was not easy work. Villanueva had to fight to overcome language difficulties, academic insecurities, mental challenges, and outright prejudice and discrimination. Part academic treatise, part memoir, Villanueva's story leaves us at once saddened, moved, depressed, thoughtful, and sometimes even hopeful. There are no easy answers to the problems of race. We are forever struggling to mediate our differences. Villanueva tries to help us grapple with difference, to make some sense of it, to learn to value it:

> What the basic writers lacked was experience with the elaborated code, a code separated from literate written discourse by little more than minor conventions [. . .]. We can introduce students to texts, read texts aloud, and nevertheless meet political aims and students' desires for an education that might provide the way for better lives. [. . .] basic writers can be encouraged to develop and to trust their oral and their literate ways while continuing to communicate the struggles entailed in being other-cultural and outside the middle class. (115)

Villanueva's book is a call to help students on the margins, those somehow marked as "different" or "unacceptable." Edith Burford's book, *Investigating the Reasons University Students in South Central United States Have to Retake First Year English Composition*, answers that call in resounding fashion. Her study is both groundbreaking and important, providing one of the few good pictures we have of teaching Mexican American students in a uniquely homogenous setting.

Edith Burford teaches the very students about whom Villanueva is so concerned. She teaches in deep south Texas, at a university in the Lower Rio Grande Valley which people refer to as a "Mexican" university, not only because of where the university is geographically located but also because the student-body is 80% Hispanic (6). The university's nickname shows how little acceptance these Hispanic/Mexican American students (Burford interchanges the two terms) have been granted.

> Villanueva knows the history of bias Burford's students face all too well:
> I think of those who try to calm others by saying that it takes two generations for ghetto dwellers to move on. This has been the pattern for immigrants. But what then do we do with the African American or the Latino, especially the Mexican-American, on American soil, in American society, far longer than two generations? What happens to them—to *us*—those of us who are of color, those of us normally labeled 'minority'? (24)

Burford's students fall into this category of "minority" and so, as Villanueva claims, they must always fight for acceptance and are forever being labeled, or labeling themselves, as not quite good enough, not credible, not worthy:

> His work has him festering in insecurity. There is grantsmanship. There is publication. There is still the dissertation. There is teaching graduate courses on writing when he still doesn't believe he knows how to write, when he is not legitimate, still fearing that he might not become legitimate, certified, the Ph.D. [. . .] In the fifteen years since Victor first entered the University, the seven years active as a professional, he has yet to meet another Puerto Rican Professor of Rhetoric and Composition. [. . .] 'We've got to keep an eye out for these people. They gotten so much handed to them that they might not know their own limitations.' Tokenism, not competence, is assumed. (117-119)

Villanueva wants us to see that for the Mexican-American, the African-American, the Asian-American, the *different*, there is never total acceptance. No credential or degree or amount of money ever seems to be enough to erase that smudge of bias. And so too many people of color live in a borderland, caught between the world of their home culture and the world of whiteness that never quite lets them in.

In the first chapter of her book, Burford explorers the difficulties of living in a borderland, both the metaphorical racial borderland as well as the geographical borderland between Mexico and the United States. Burford traces out a history of the region and discusses the health, drug, and infant-mortality problems of a United States that is nothing like the privileged one in which most of us live.

Burford then brings these borderland problems home to the English department and the composition classroom by pointing out that "there is a history of a high rate of students repeating First-Year Composition because they did not pass the course with a C or better, or because they dropped the course mid-semester" (5). Calculating this failure rate at a stunning 65% (1), Burford aims her study at understanding the cause of this failure rate and also unpacking the reasons why so many Hispanic students in particular are failing, or being stopped from passing, composition. In short, she asks us to follow her on a guided exploration of the borderlands, looking to see what barriers prevent young Hispanic students from crossing over to the land of promise.

In the second chapter of her book, Burford cites Kay Losey's research on the problem of silencing Mexican American students. Burford then reviews the current literature looking for ways to counteract this silencing. Burford explores current research into teaching and learning styles that are suitable for Mexican American students. She also discusses research on cultural identity that is useful for teachers seeking to understand the difficulties Mexican American students may face in the classroom. Especially important in this chapter is Burford's discussion of the common Initiation-Response-Evaluation (IRE) teaching style that "tends to favor some students over others because of its familiarity in the homes primarily of mainstream, middle-class students. This creates a distinct disadvantage to and effectively silences those for whom the IRE teaching pattern is not standard form" (13). Most relevant of all to Burford's later findings is her discussion contrasting field dependent and field independent learners (19-20). Burford points out that most Hispanic students tend to be field dependent learners who are group oriented due to their cultural background. Unfortunately, says Burford, most Anglo American classrooms tend to be designed to suit the learning styles of field independent learners who are usually more competitive and individualistic. Burford discusses in detail this conflict as it has been explored in the current research literature. In summary, Burford's survey of current research helps readers to understand the various challenges Mexican American learners face in many classrooms as well as why these students are so often driven into silence.

Burford uses the third chapter of her book to outline her research methodology. She followed a qualitative research approach with a focus on survey and interview data collection methods. Burford gathered information from students enrolled in first-year composition at her university as well as faculty members teaching that course. Burford gave a general survey to 282 students (43) and then held detailed interviews with 37 of these students (53). She also surveyed six and interviewed four (101) of the composition teachers instructing these students.

Burford focused both her survey questions and interview questions on issues of teaching style, learning style, and cultural identity, allowing readers to draw connections back to those same issues in her literature review. Chapter three of this volume also includes a detailed discussion of the types of questions Burford asked of the students and teachers participating in her study. In general, Burford's questions to the students "focused on aspects of teaching that assist learning academic writing" (53) while her questions of the teachers "asked how they approach teaching essay writing, how they demonstrated the process of writing, and how they deal with the variety of learning styles" (54).

While such participant self-reports are always subjective, Burford nevertheless appears to have succeeded in collecting authentic research data from her participants. One mark of the trustworthiness of her data is her observation that, "the responses of both students and faculty are reliable because some of the replies were belligerent, accusative, but they seemed honest" (41-42). Burford is clearly a researcher who is not afraid to hear unpleasant truths, and this makes her study all the more valuable to teachers and composition scholars who want to learn new information about how best to teach composition to Mexican American students.

In the fourth chapter of her book, Burford guides us through a detailed analysis of her data. She takes us first through the survey data and then through the interview data, balancing her analysis between student and teacher input. It is clear from the chapter that Burford has been exacting in combing through her data. And this analysis yields some valuable results. For instance, Burford notes that 70% of the students reported that they preferred to work in groups when doing assignments (57). Burford notes that this finding seems to match the highly community-based cultural background of her students. The finding also highlights the potential clash between Mexican American student learning styles and the classrooms in which they find themselves; the field dependent versus field independent learning differences Burford carefully examined in chapter two.

Along with the basic statistical responses to her survey questions, Burford includes some highly illuminating quotes from the student surveys. For example, in response to a question about why students preferred certain teachers, one student said, "He taught in a way we understood. He used our language rather than being proper all the time" (61). Burford links this statement to the literature on how Mexican American students understand the concept of teacher. Even more illuminating, though disheartening, is a comment by one student in answer to the question why some teachers were not liked: "I dropped the course because she did not explain anything and she was kind of racist about Mexicans" (63). Such comments, both positive and negative, help us to gain a better picture of the vii

context in which Mexican American students are struggling to learn composition in this setting.

While Burford takes pains to cover both the student and teacher data, the student-based data is easily the most compelling. It is a credit to Burford as a researcher that she has been able to collect such valuable, honest, and intellectually arresting material for study. Far too little of this research data has been available to us in the past. In fact, one of the greatest values of Burford's book is that it gives these Mexican American students some small opportunities to speak. As one student tells us: "My mother is very proud since I am the first generation to attend [college]. It's what they have always wanted. No one can take your education from you" (73). Any study like Burford's that can give direct voice to Mexican American students' beliefs and concerns is a study well worth reading.

In the fifth and final chapter of her book, Burford uses her study data to answer her central research question: Why do so many Hispanic students have to retake first year English composition? As I have noted, in contrast to most United States universities, at Burford's institution, Hispanic students make up a vast majority of the student body (over 80%). In such an atmosphere, we might expect and certainly would hope for a high success rate for the Hispanic students taking first year English composition. Unfortunately, this is not the case. Sadly, almost 65% of the students taking composition fail to complete the course with at least a grade of C at Burford's university (1). After hundreds of surveys and numerous interviews, Burford tries to shed some light on why all these Hispanic students are having to retake composition.

Burford's analysis does not point to the cultural mismatch one might expect given that the faculty teaching composition are Anglo American and the students are primarily Mexican American. In their survey and interview responses, both teachers and students told Burford that the high failure rate was due to students being lazy and not taking responsibility for their education (122). But Burford wisely pushes her analysis beyond this overly simplistic explanation. Instead, Burford offers an explanation of the problem grounded on learning styles theory. Consistent with current research literature, Burford says the data she gathered in her surveys and interviews of the Mexican American students indicated that most of these students were field dependent learners while the data on these students' teachers showed that the teachers were employing teaching styles aimed at field independent learners (122). Burford claims that it is this learning style mismatch, not a cultural mismatch, which creates classroom conflict, student rebellion, and ultimately the high failure rate that necessitates so many Mexican American students to retake composition at this institution. It is here that Burford says teachers must focus their pedagogical reform efforts, particularly on assisting "those students who have been in this country long enough to no longer be Field Dependent, but [. . .] have not evolved enough to be Field Independent. They are somewhere in between, Field-Intermediate" (122). Burford claims that these Field-Intermediate students are the ones having to retake composition, and she urges teachers and researchers to find a way to help this group of students become successful.

Burford concludes her fifth chapter with a discussion of a number of interesting future studies that might be done as a follow-up to her work. Her calls for more research should be quite helpful to other scholars working in this same area of investigation.

Composition scholars will also be happy to find that Burford has included a current, detailed, and highly useful works cited on issues of teaching and learning styles, cultural identity, and studies of Mexican American students. This excellent works cited rounds out Burford's book nicely and accentuates the overall value of her contribution to the field.

Edith Burford's *Investigating the Reasons University Students in South Central United States Have to Retake First Year English Composition* is a fine book. It shows dedication not only to scholarly excellence, but also to quality teaching. Edith Burford is clearly a woman who cares about her students, and she has used her research to listen to students the way any good teacher does. We are fortunate to have this opportunity to hear what Mexican American students and their teachers have to tell us about improving composition teaching. Clearly we need many more such studies, and Burford's work, following humbly in the footsteps of Victor Villanueva, helps pave the way. As we move further into the Twenty-first Century, we can use Edith Burford's research as a stepping stone on our path to learning how we must reshape composition if we ever hope to make it a course where Mexican American students, and indeed all students, can find their voices.

Works Cited

Losey, Kay M. Listen to the Silences. Mexican American Interaction in the Composition Classroom and the Community. Norwood, NJ: Ablex Publishing Corp., 1997.

Villanueva, Victor, Jr. Bootstraps. From an American Academic of Color. Urbana, IL: National Council of Teachers of English., 1993.

Acknowledgments

I would like to acknowledge and thank the faculty and students at the University who participated in the research. In particular, I would like to thank Dr. Beatrice Mendez Newman for being my mentor when I began my research, and to Dr. Rodolfo Rocha, Dean of the College of Arts and Humanities, for supporting my research and encouraging me.

In addition, I would like to thank my husband, Kenneth, for his support and all the time he spent proofreading and giving pep talks. Also I want to thank all four of my children and their families for their interest in this project. But especially, I would like to acknowledge my two daughters who live in Texas and their children, my grandchildren, for their special interest and support. Additionally, I would like to thank my many friends whose ever constant encouragement and belief in me kept me going toward my goal.

Chapter 1. The Problem and Its Significance

Introduction to the History of the Area

The University is located in the southern tip of Texas in the Lower Rio Grande Valley. This University is second to a Florida university in total Hispanic enrollment at four-year colleges. [The University] has 10,507 Hispanics out of 12,569 total students. Florida International University in Miami has 16,469 out of 31,293 total students. [University of Texas] UT El Paso was listed third in the nation" (qtd. in Arevelo 4). Although Florida International University in Miami has more Hispanic students than the University, the ratio of Hispanics in Miami's student body is less. Miami's Hispanic ratio to total student body is 52.5%, while the University's ratio of Hispanics out of the total student body is 83.6%. However, the vast majority of all the University's faculty is of Anglo-Saxon/European descent.

In the English department, there are forty full-time faculty, but only five of them are Hispanic and only two of the Hispanics teach First-Year Composition. Moreover, there is a history of a high rate of students repeating First-Year Composition because they did not pass the course with a C or better, or because they dropped the course mid-semester. According to students who self declared while being surveyed, 65% of the students enrolled in English 1301 First-Year Composition did not complete the course or did not earn a passing grade of C or better. In the English 1301 First-Year Composition, the student population in each of the classes is usually 90-95% Hispanic, but the teachers of this course are usually Anglo-Saxon/European heritage. This statistic lumped together those students who dropped the course, withdrew from the University, or did not earn a passing grade. Since the University student body is 83.6% Hispanic and the faculty is 49.75% Caucasian, 39.6% Hispanic, and 10.75% other, the faculty does not reflect the student population (University 2000 Fact Book 167).

Because the University is located in the Lower Rio Grande Valley of Texas, it is known as a "Mexican" university, even though Texas is part of the U.S. In fact, the Valley has an identity problem, even with Texans. Unfortunately, most Americans and many Texans seem to "forget" that the southern boundary of Texas does not stop at Corpus Christi and the Nueces River, but it continues another 150 miles south to the Rio Grande River. The area between the Nueces River and the Rio Grande River contains nine counties, but the portion considered the Lower Rio Grande Valley includes the three southernmost counties: Cameron County which has Brownsville as its largest city, Willacy County which is just north of Cameron County has Raymondville as its largest city, Hidalgo County which is west of those two counties has McAllen as its largest city. These three counties are often referred to as The Valley.

It may surprise some people that the Rio Grande River has not always been the southern Texas border. Until the United States-Mexico War (1846-48), the southmost border of Texas was the Nueces River which runs from just south of Corpus Christi west across the state to Laredo. After the fall of the Alamo in today's San Antonio, Sam Houston captured Mexico's General Santa Ana's army at San Jacinto near today's city of Houston. To save his own life after the Battle of the Alamo, Santa Ana signed the Treaty of Velasco on May 14, 1836, and the secret Compromise of 1850 (McDonald TexasEscapes.com). "The treaty called for Mexican recognition of the independence of the Republic of Texas, with the Rio Grande as its southern boundary, rather than the traditional boundary of the Rio Nueces" (Miller and Almaraz qtd. in Cisneros 28). With this shift of boundary, it became a case of the boundary crossing the people, rather than the people crossing the boundary (Miller and Almaraz qtd. in Cisneros 31).

Unrest and uncertainty continued in the newly acquired land of the Republic of Texas, as well as the unstable government of Mexico. This led to a plan for a number of counties from the Nueces River south into northern Mexico to form a new country. Tired of the government in Austin ignoring their needs, some Texans not connected with the government of the new republic became involved early in 1839 in a movement for the organization of a new country called the Republic of the Rio Grande. It gained enough support for a convention, a provisional government, and named Laredo as the capital (Johnson 31). The Mexican government fought the new Republic, and Texas did not offer much support. So on November 6, 1840, the Republic dissolved, and was "never again to be revived. The Republic had lasted 283 stormy, turbulent days" (Johnson 31). However, after "the signing of the Guadalupe Hidalgo Treaty in 1848 at the end of the United States-Mexico War and the Gadsden Purchase in 1853 fixed the U.S.-Mexico border [. . .] [as] [t]he Rio Grande [river], or Rio Bravo, as it is called in Mexico, [. . .]" (Smithsonian 51) and confirmed the region as South Texas.

The shifting of the boundary, along with the ranchers forcing the shift of the Trans-Nueces Watershed and creation of the Rio Grande Watershed in 1850, created mixed loyalties. With this mix of loyalties came conflict: conflict of politics, economic methods, and lifestyles which continue to this day.

> Our southern frontier is not simply American on one side and Mexican on the other. It is a third country with its own identity. This third country [. . .] has its own outlaws, its own police officers and its own policy makers. Its food, its language, its music are its own. Even its economy is unique. It's a colony unto itself [. . .] (T. Miller xii)

But life on the border only appears tranquil. "Conflict–cultural, economic, and physical–has been a way of life along the border between Mexico and the United states, and it is in the so-called Nueces-Rio Grande strip where its patterns were first established" (Paredes qtd. in Smithsonian). Life on the U.S.-Mexico border has a distinct undercurrent.

> It gnaws at one's consciousness like a fear of rabid dogs and coyotes. Beneath every action lies the context of border life. And one must see that undergirding for what it is–the pain and sorrow of daily reminders that here disease runs rampant, here drug crimes take a daily toll, here infant mortality rates run as high or higher than those of Third World countries [. . .] (Cantu qtd. in Smithsonian)

In many parts of the Valley today, this undercurrent is still evident. Even though the State of Texas has outlawed the sale of substandard property, some real estate salespeople still sell to recent immigrants property with no sewage, electricity or running water available. Locally these neighborhoods are called <u>colonias</u>; in other border areas, they are called <u>barrios</u>.

The primary language of the area had been Spanish, but as a result of the boundary shift, English became the official language. Of the counties that comprise the Valley, 84.7% of the general population have Spanish surnames, most are of Mexican descent, but some are of Central and South American heritage (McAllen Chamber of Commerce). However, not all people with Hispanic surnames speak Spanish. About 2% claim to speak no Spanish. Of course, many people without Spanish surnames also speak Spanish (Amastae 5).

Problem

There is a history of a high rate of students repeating First-Year Composition because they did not pass the course with a C or better, or because they dropped the course mid-semester. In the English 1301 First-Year Composition classes, the student population in each of the classes can be 90-95% Hispanic. Unfortunately, the University Registrar's Office does not maintain statistics of students who fail or drop classes for any class in any discipline. Further, the English department only records data for classes as a whole, not for individual students. The only way that a professor can know if a student has repeated an English course is at the beginning of the semester when the Registrar sends every teacher a history of English courses taken and grades earned by each student in each class. The purpose of the history is to ensure that all students enrolled in the class have taken and passed all prerequisites with a grade of C or better. However, conventional wisdom states that students whose first language is not English will not succeed in school. "In fact, one of the most common strategies for dealing with these students, flunking them, is also the least effective" (Perez 151).

Teachers should learn more about minority cultures beyond their traditional dress, food, and holidays. Those who have ethnic minorities in their classrooms should take sociocultural factors into consideration. Miville, Koonce, Darlington, and Whitlock studied African Americans and Mexican Americans to learn if there is a relationship between how these minorities and whites relate to themselves and their cultural, racial, and ego identities (208). The researchers found that "both African Americans and Mexican Americans have developed [. . .] identities based on their respective group's history of exposure to widespread and continuing discrimination" (216). Results showed that for both groups to achieve ego identity, or a positive sense of self, they had to achieve a positive racial or cultural identity. For African Americans' ego identity meant a naive racial world view with a conforming racial identity (217). However, the Mexican American ego identity combined with cultural identity but less than for African Americans (217). Thus, both groups self-reported race-ethnicity as important or very important to their identity, whereas White American participants rated identity as least important (209). Instructors should recognize these sociocultural differences and address them in the classroom, rather than treating these students as some teachers do. As Salili, Chiu, and Hong state, "Many sociocultural factors contribute to school failures [and drop outs]. Among them are diversity in cultural background, limited knowledge of the mainstream language, and poverty" (3).

Previously, most student retention research has only studied mainstream white students (Urdan 183). Thus, the aspirations of the subjects researched may differ from those compared with in a later study. "For example, students who are raised in a culture where competition between peers is seen as a healthy, normal part of development may perceive and interpret performance goal messages differently than those from cultures that place greater emphasis on cooperation" (184). Likewise, some cultures encourage academic independence, but professors often require students to get into groups for group projects or to read work produced by members of the group and give feedback. Ofttimes, students feel conflict when teachers make this assignment. "[C]ross-cultural psychologists have argued that the construal of the self is culturally bound and takes a different meaning within a western and an eastern perspective" (Volet 312-13). In other words, sense of the self is interconnected with ethnic identity, varies from culture to culture, and especially, cross-culturally from the eastern and western society.

> Western cultures are characterized by an *independent* sense of self - a self that exists apart from all others, and defines all others separately from it, no matter how close their relationship is to the self. In contrast, Eastern cultures are characterized by an *interdependent* sense of self - a self that includes not only you but your family and friends and society, a self that cannot be defined independent of the roles and relationships it exists in. Thus, failure in a Western society is a reflection on you (the independent self), but failure in an Eastern society can be viewed by virtue of the interdependent conception of self, as a reflection on all those with whom you share an important relationship, particularly family members. (Grant and Dweck 208)

Consequently, in the multi-cultural college classroom, much care must be taken to address the many variables of ethnicity, and sociocultural identity. For this reason, it has been popularly thought by many that if African Americans, or Hispanics, or Asians could be the majority of the student population in a university, or in effect have their own schools, that those students would experience greater academic success. Thus, since Hispanics are the majority of the student population in the University, then the students should be able to have a high pass rate in the First-Year Composition course. Hispanics should excel at this University. Why do so many Hispanic students have to repeat this course in a "Mexican University"? Is there clash of cultures with the predominately Anglo American faculty with almost totally Hispanic student body? Is this just an assumption from an outside observer? Or is this also the perception of the faculty and students in the English department? What do the students and faculty perceive is the reason for the low pass rate in this course at this University? A review of the literature, study, methodology and results follow.

Chapter 2. Review of the Literature

Many university and college campuses have experienced an influx of U.S.-educated nonnative speakers of English. Students may come to college with almost native speaking skills yet they have marginal literacy skills. Harklau, Losey, and Siegal refer to these U.S.-educated learners of ESL as Generation 1.5 (qtd. in Khirallah 600). The instructor needs to be very sensitive to the emotional climate of the classroom. It is essential that teachers look for students who appear apprehensive or anxious, and make sure that a quiet student has not been inadvertently made to feel excluded or ignored, or as Losey calls it "silenced" (2). Mexican Americans are often silenced by instructors overlooking them both in the classroom and in the community (1).

> [This] community, like many across California and the country, has a striking history of silencing its ethnic minorities–literally and metaphorically. [. . .] Mexican Americans have been silenced for hundreds of years on a variety of fronts–political, economic, cultural, and ethnic. They have been denied the right to vote and to political representation, to their property and to fair wages, to celebrate traditional holidays, and to live free of prejudice and bigotry. The teacher [. . .] and her students have spent nearly 20 years in this climate. Living in a community that silences Mexican Americans at every opportunity, and has for generations, creates a context in which the silence of Mexican Americans seems normal–to both Anglo Americans and many Mexican Americans. (Losey 2-3)

The instructor will want to recognize and to call on all of her students to make the classroom feel safe for all students. "When the classroom feels comfortable enough for each person to relax, then students from various backgrounds can take the risk of expressing their views, resulting in a richer blend of perspectives" (Hughes, Romeo, and Romeo 411). So how do they do this? By being particularly cognizant of their teaching styles, their student's learning styles, and their student's culture and ethnicity.

Teaching Style

A teaching style may be defined as a behavior, rather than a methodology (K. Dunn and Frazier 347-367). Behavior, in this sense, is the manner in which a teacher conducts her class. Erickson and Erickson assert there are certain skills that college instructors will find essential to become effective teachers.

> Among the skills [. . .] are providing introductions which arouse interest, and suggest an organizational framework for instruction; using examples, anecdotes, or illustrations to explain and clarify subject matter; asking questions to stimulate and direct thinking; providing variety in materials and methods; communicating respect and concern for students; constructing valid and reliable examinations; and giving feedback which enables students to monitor their progress. (58)

Losey discovered that students' reaction to assignments differed according to gender. She found that when assigned essays, Mexican American men tended to procrastinate more than other students; however, Mexican American women turned in their homework, revised essays and wrote well (132). Although both sexes appeared to have just as many outside responsibilities, the women completed and turned in more assignments than the men. "In comparison to the women, the men were silenced in interaction around course assignments" (134). The Mexican American men seemed to be intimidated at putting their thoughts in writing and thus were silenced. Still, study results showed that Mexican Americans overall wrote more revisions than the Anglo American subjects, and most of those were written by Mexican American women (145). While the Mexican American men were silenced by writing, the Mexican American women were silenced during classroom discussion. The women did speak some, but not as often nor as loudly as the men. The women seemed to remain silent in deference to the men (156). The Mexican American students in Losey's study were silenced through an interplay of several factors including ethnicity, gender, and linguistic barriers.

> This silencing interfered with Mexican American students' access to the same educational benefits as their Anglo American counterparts. In general, the Mexican American students–male and female–interacted less frequently than the Anglo American students. The Mexican American men were silenced in written interaction, and the women in classroom talk. Although both Mexican American and Anglo American women were relatively silent during whole class discussions compared with the men of their particular ethnic group, there was a greater discrepancy between the interaction of the Mexican American men and women than between Anglo American men and women. Moreover, the Anglo American women, although less verbal than the Anglo American men, were still more talkative than the Mexican American men or women, thereby creating an ethnic and gender hierarchy of interaction in the classroom. (193)

Although Losey referred to Hispanics only in her research mentioned above, other minorities have also been silenced. One teaching style often used both in the classroom and the mainstream, middle-class home to elicit student response is the Initiation-Response-Evaluation (IRE). In the classroom, the teacher has control of the topic and students have little opportunity to ask questions or take part in class discussion. Moreover, this affords Non-Native Speakers little opportunity to use the target language in the classroom. This indicates that the IRE teaching pattern tends to favor some students over others because of its familiarity in the home primarily of mainstream, middle-class students. This creates a distinct disadvantage to and effectively silences those for whom the IRE teaching pattern is not standard form, especially among "working class Anglo and rural black families, Native Americans, ethnic Hawaiians, inner city black youths, and [. . .] bilingual Chicanos" (Losey 10).

Learning Style

A teacher needs to take many variables into consideration when choosing the teaching style to use in class. Teaching styles go along with learning styles which are the cognitive styles and strategies used when learning a task "irrespective of learning task differences" (Frisby 536). Sims and Sims point out there is body of definitions of learning style which is "often used interchangeably with cognitive style or learning ability" (xii). They define learning styles as "characteristic cognitive, affective, and psychological behaviors that serve as relatively stable indicators of how learners perceive, interact with, and respond to the learning environment" (Sims and Sims 50). According to Messick,

> an individual's cognitive style reflects 'stable attitudes, preferences, or habitual strategies determining a person's typical modes of perceiving, remembering, thinking, and problem solving.' [. . .] [C]ognitive styles reflect individual differences in how information and experience is organized and processed. (qtd. in Frisby 536)

Further, "[c]ognitive styles are information processing habits of representing the learner's typical mode of perceiving, thinking, problem solving, and remembering" (Sims and Sims 50). Learning occurs through the sensory channels or pathways through which students give, receive, and store information using their perception, memory and all of their senses. The strength of these traits and race are not related because culture will influence an individual's approach to learning, and generalizations cannot be made (Reiff 17, 18). A "learning style is the way students begin to concentrate on, process, internalize, and remember new and difficult academic information" (R. Dunn 8).

Another definition of learning styles are the "unique ways whereby an individual gathers and processes information and are the means by which an individual prefers to learn" (Davidson 36). Frisby gives two other definitions of learning styles:

> Schmeck defined learning style generally as the cognitive style that a person manifests when confronted with a learning task [. . .]. (qtd. in Frisby 536)

In the learning style studies that were conducted from the 1950s throughout the 1980s, most of the college and university studies used Caucasian subjects. When diversity became an issue on college campuses during the 1980s, the research in these learning style studies came into question (Sims and Sims 37). Five major cultural groups exist in the United States today: Native American, Hispanic American, African American, Asian American, and European American. "Although each cultural group encompassed multiple [learning] styles, patterns emerged that suggested elements within each cultural group. [. .. .] [T]here was great diversity within each cultural group. Research indicates that the differences *within* each cultural group were greater than the differences *between* cultural groups" (R. Dunn 17). Consequently, a cultural approach to teaching a class of college students cannot be successful unless each student's individual strengths are evaluated and addressed (17).

However, cultural differentiation determines the cross-cultural application of general learning principles known as "Ferguson's Law" (Frisby 536). Specifically, "Ferguson's law states that 'cultural factors prescribe what shall be learned and at what age, consequently different cultural environments lead to the development of different patterns of ability'" (536). Some researchers began "comparative research on psychoeducational characteristics of different 'cultures' [. . .] such as Native-Americans, Mexican-Americans, African-Americans, Asian-Americans, and Pacific Islanders" (536). Of course, these psychoeducational characteristics of learning begin in the home during infancy. "[C]ulture plays an important part in determining how students have learned to learn at home. When that style is not congruent with the school learning style, the student is expected to change his/her style to fit that of the school" (Swisher and Deyhle 345). Cultures have distinct learning patterns, "but the great variation among individuals within groups means that educators must use diverse teaching strategies with all students" (Guild 16). This is a difficult daily cultural adjustment to the culture of the school and its teachers (19).

When teachers are aware of the learning needs of their students, they can adapt their teaching style to meet the needs of their class which increases learning and understanding (Davidson 36-38). While this is valid, Frisby "finds legitimate disagreement among theorists as to its instructional implications" (547). Some learning style theorists argue that instructional methods should match students' learning style, while other theorists contend that students should be more flexible and adapt to the teacher's teaching style. Davidman maintains that when teaching and learning styles match, the student may benefit in the short term, "but such an approach is more than likely to stunt students' intellectual development in the long run" (qtd. in Frisby 357). No matter which teaching style is used, teachers want to focus on the content to be learned, the student's current abilities, and the demands of the task (Stahl 27-31, Henak 23-28, Dillon 503-514, Rodrigues, Bu, and Min 23).

Many students who graduate from high school and enter college or university are underprepared to successfully perform in first semester courses. Many academics fail to associate a student's performance levels with their cultural background, and cultural learning styles (Kolodny par. 1-6). Because the various cultures have different value systems, each culture defines for itself the style of learning within its community. The mainstream White American culture values "independence, analytic thinking, objectivity, and accuracy. These values translate into learning experiences that focus on competition, information, tests and grades, and linear logic. These patterns are prevalent in most American schools" (Guild 17-18). Teachers who have ethnic minorities in their classrooms will want to take these sociodemographic and sociocultural factors into consideration.

Furthermore there is a constant influx of Hispanic immigrants, both legal and illegal, both from Mexico and through Mexico, from Central and South America. It would be a mistake to lump all Hispanics into one group. Most of the newer immigrants could be classified as Traditional; that is their primary language is Spanish, both immediate and extended family are very important, adults are primary role models and a major teaching element in both family and community, and they follow Mexican Catholic traditions (Jimenez 16).

After a family has been in the US for a period of time, it becomes Dualistic; the adults speak Spanish, but the children speak both English and Spanish. The immediate family remains very important. In addition to the extended family, peer groups grow in influence, and adults in the community become less of a role model. Religion becomes a mixture of Mexican and American Catholic traditions (Jimenez 16).

Most of the students in English 1301 First-Year Composition fall in the Dualistic category, but many fall in the third classification, Assimilated. In this group, the primary language is English, the immediate family is still a dynamic force in their lives, but the clan effect dissipates and no longer has a strong influence on relationships. Religious ties change to American Catholic or Protestant, and students become more competitive and achievement oriented as their Anglo-American counterparts are (Jimenez 16). While a general theory will always have individual exceptions, most recent Hispanic immigrants use the psychological cognitive learning style of Field Dependent. As they become assimilated into the American culture, they develop into Field Independent learners, a characteristic which Anglo-Americans tend to exhibit.

The concept of Field Dependence was first described by Herman Witkin in 1941 (Goodenough 5) and researched more by Gestalt psychologists in the 1940s and 1950s. Originally, the term "field" meant the field of vision of the subject being studied because the study researched the subject's body posture in relation to visual cues (Witkin and Goodenough 8, 14). Later, researchers included other stimuli as articulation and other noises and distraction. During the 1970s, the studies turned to the cultural impact on learning styles and field dependence. Among the groups studied were various American cultures, including Italian American, Mexican American, Cuban American, Colombian American, Peruvian American, African American, Anglo American, and others (91). Witkin defined field dependent as people who relied on visual or external cues, and field independent as people who relied on internal or body (gut related) cues (Ming and Patty 183; Goodenough 6). "Field dependent individuals are more group-oriented and cooperative and less competitive than field independent individuals" (Griggs and R. Dunn 14). Witkin noted that those two groups could fall at the extremes of a continuum, but there are learners who fall in the middle. These learners became the "field intermediate" group and did not differ from the others except by degree, and moderation (Meng and Patty183).

Field independent learner:

1. is more task oriented,

2. has well developed analytical abilities,

3. is motivated by individual competition and achievement,

4. perceives the specific, then the totality

5. can work well alone,

6. is not affected as much by outside stimuli such as the instructor or the environment when solving a problem or performing a task (Jimenez 17).

Field dependent or field sensitive learner:

1. works well in groups,

2. perceives the totality, then the specific,

3. is motivated by group competition and achievement,

4. is more affected by outside stimuli such as the instructor or the environment when solving a problem or performing a task,

5. is influenced more by affective variables in learning. (Jimenez 17)

Carli, Lancia, and Paniccia found that Field Dependence and Field Independence could apply to ethnicities and cultures, too (63-83). Griggs and R. Dunn point out that research has indicated that Mexican-American and other minority students are more field dependent than nonminority students.

> Hudgens found that Hispanic middle and secondary school students were more field dependent than Anglo students; Hispanic female (and African-American male) students had a greater internal locus of control than other groups; and Hispanic male (and African-American female) students had a greater external locus of control than other groups. (B. Hudgens qtd. in Griggs and R. Dunn 14).

Ricardo Jimenez also found that Hispanics in general are field dependent learners.

Cultural Identity

As evident by Jimenez' work, Hispanic Americans are united by customs, language, religion, and values, but there is a great diversity among individuals. One of the most important qualities is commitment to family,

> which involves loyalty, a strong support system, a belief that a child's behavior reflects on the honor of the family, a hierarchical order among siblings, and a duty to care for family members. This strong sense of other-directedness conflicts with the United States mainstream emphasis on individualism. Indeed, Hispanic culture's emphasis on cooperation in the attainment of goals can result in Hispanic students' discomfort with this nation's conventional classroom competition. (Griggs and R. Dunn 12)

With a classroom of Hispanic students, there are a myriad of cultural differences within that group that can aid the teacher in selecting teaching styles. Sometimes the sociodemographic variables of the lower economic status of Hispanic students and the requisite hours of employment often result in students being underprepared for college (Canabal 157-167). Cho and Forde studied students who identified themselves as Native American, African American or Black, Mexican American or Hispanic, Asian/Pacific Islander, White or Caucasian and other ethnic groups. They found significant differences in the learning styles of the White group and with all other ethnic groups researched. There were also significant differences between students based on gender and socio-economic status (86-95). Thus, lack of preparedness often results in students experiencing frustration, stress, and discouragement. Because most professors do not, or cannot, attempt intervention to prevent drop out, the result is a high rate of attrition (Canabal 157-167, Dreher 26-29).

I am going to use the term Hispanic, rather than Latino, Chicano, Mexican American, because that is the preferred term in the area of the Lower Rio Grande Valley and the most prevalent term used in the literature. The people have a variety of histories. Some were native born because their families have been in what is now the United States territories since the sixteenth century. Some were born in Central or South America or Mexico and are now naturalized citizens. Others are in the US illegally or maybe recent immigrants and are undocumented (Rosaldo and Flores 59). A Latina, or Hispanic, woman explained her connection to her culture in this way,

> "Culture gives us a sense of unity, of connectedness, a vision of our identity," explains a Latino woman [. . .]. "The difficulty is trying to pinpoint what we mean by culture. It isn't simply language, community, the arts, religion, history. [. . .] It is a little of each, and all at the same time. We all know what it is, but we can't explain it. It makes us closer to our brothers and sisters; it makes us disregard the differences when it comes to the tough things of life; it's like a unity within the difference." Culture provides, then a sense of belonging to a community, a feeling of entitlement, the energy to face everyday adversities, and a rationale for resistance to a larger world in which members of minority groups feel like aliens in spite of being citizens. (Silvestrini 43)

Ethnic identity, racial identity, and cultural identity have intertwined definitions. Ethnic identity is often described as having two components: content and salience.

> The content of ethnic identity refers to the customs, language, behaviors, music, literature, heroes, values, and worldview that a group with a common ethnic heritage shares. The salience of ethnic identity describes the degree to which membership in the group and the content of ethnic identity are important to the individual's sense of self. (Ortiz 69)

Racial identity comprises both the content and salience of ethnic identity, but "adds the process by which individuals come to terms with the consequences of that group's place in society. Realizing that racism exists and developing a positive self-concept as a member of a racial group are emphasized in these models" (69).

> Cultural identity [. . .] is a broader term that encompasses racial, ethnic, and cultural groups. Cultural identity is very similar to ethnic and racial identity, but the commonality does not have to be ethnic. Groups with common values, customs, practices, and experiences might [. . .] often experience oppression in ways similar to those described by racial identity models. (Ortiz 69-70)

Culture identity then is "contrasting 'our' beliefs and behavior, which are examples to be followed, with 'theirs' which must be avoided because they seem strange and alien" (Silvestrini 47).

Accompanying identity is enculturation and acculturation. Ortiz defines enculturation as "the socialization process by which individuals acquire the host of culturation and psychological qualities that are necessary to function as a member of one's group (70). She defines acculturation as "the product of culture learning that occurs as a result of contact between the members of two or more culturally distinct groups, a process of attitudinal and behavioral change undergone, willingly or unwillingly, by individuals who reside in multicultural societies (70). An acculturation study focused on Mexican Americans' cultural changes over generations of United States residence and found that while cultural changes occurred, ethnic identity did not change. The subjects rated their perceived satisfaction degree of comfort in both Mexican and Anglo American cultures (Montgomery 202). The outcome of the study showed an "acculturation stress" among Mexican Americans that could result in possible health concerns (219). Acculturation stress could vary within the diverse groups that exist inside of ethnic groups. For example, Native Americans have separate tribes, but within each tribe is a distinct heritage. Asian Americans and Hispanics hail from many different countries which "differ within and between specific national groups by generational status (time in the United States)" (Ortiz 70).

For this reason, teachers should consider the lack of preparedness and the elements which differentiate the many individuals of the same cultural group:

self identification (e.g., Latinos who identify themselves as Mexican Americans versus Chicanos). This difference in self identification usually reflects a distinct sociopolitical perspective.

race (e.g., white Cubans who share a similar Spanish language and culture with black Cubans). This confusion of culture and race is common. Culture is not always affiliated with race.

country of origin (e.g., Indo-Chinese from Laos versus Cambodia or Latinos from Mexico versus El Salvador). These groups may have a common global culture but often vary significantly in language, ideology, and microcultural aspects.

generation in the United States (e.g., fifth generation Mexican Americans in California versus recent immigrants). Though similar in cultural heritage, individuals would vary tremendously.

level of assimilation (e.g., Native Americans who live on reservations versus Native Americans with no ties to traditional lifestyles). Though members of the same minority grouping, vast differences would be evident.

socio-economic status (e.g., middle class African Americans versus poor inner city African Americans). This is one of the most important variables, because it determines much in the way of lifestyle, education, and power.

language(s) proficiency (e.g., bilingual Puerto Ricans versus monolingual (English or Spanish only) Puerto Ricans). In addition to fluency, there is also the issue of how languages are used by the various Puerto Rican communities. (Garza 25-26)

Students are generally capable even if they have language use problems. However, the problem may not lie with teaching or learning styles, but with a student's cultural identity. Raul Ybarra studied two students and found that their classroom participation problems proceeded from cultural identity. One of the students in the study did not feel that she had a cultural identity. She did not feel Argentinian as her father, Ecuadorian as her mother, nor could she identify with her "Anglo–mainstream instructors" (161). In fact, she did not feel that she had a culture. The second student did not feel she had a right to voice her opinions. Previous teachers had convinced her that the only valid opinion was the instructor's. Further, she "equated speaking out in class with getting punished" (164).

Because teachers often do not understand minority cultures, many students may become frustrated, angry, suspicious, and mistrust school systems. This attitude is not unusual with Hispanic and other minority students. Many students believe that something is wrong with them when they cannot please instructors, so they feel their only option is to drop the class, or to drop out of school, although not all students do. Teachers often do not understand who their students are, where they come from, or their culture (Ybarra 168). It is essential that instructors not only hear what their students tell them, but really listen to them. Ortiz and Garcia wrote, "When teachers fail to recognize the cultural differences among learning styles, students react in negative ways to the instruction" (qtd. in Oxford and Anderson 201). The usual student reaction is to drop the class.

Angela McGlynn, a professor with Mercer County (NJ) Community College, reports that "statistics of the U.S. Census Bureau, [show that] only 6.9 percent of Hispanic women have completed college. The completion rate of Black women is 10.2 percent, and that of white women, 17.6% (12). Further, she states the Hispanic group is diverse and "varies according to nationality. Per the Census Bureau, immigrants from Cuba, Chile, and Argentina are more likely than those from Mexico to have at least a high school diploma" (12). McGlynn's solution is for the faculty to be proactive in keeping Hispanic females in school and to incorporate the writing of Hispanic women into First-Year English readings (12-14).

Miglietti and Strange studied whether a student who delays higher education versus the student who comes directly from high school has different classroom expectations and experiences (1-19). Hutchinson and Beadle studied whether gender has an impact on learning style (405-418). "The key here may be developing a range of teaching style options, some of which may be most appropriate [. . .] at the beginning of the term, and others that may serve students better as they gain [. . .] confidence [. . .]" (Miglietti and Strange 15). Cultural awareness and learning styles may cause teachers to realize that not every one learns as the teacher does. This realization may cause teachers to use various teaching styles (Mangan par. 1-8). A multicultural classroom requires embracing the diversity, and show respect by trying to correctly pronounce names. An example is not changing Jorge to George or Martinez' to Martin'ez (Perez 151). Another way to show respect to student diversity is not to try to force them to give up their language. In many cases, it is language that is their only connection to their culture. Also, "cognitive and academic skills transfer across languages [. . .]. A curriculum that uses content from a variety of cultures presents a more accurate version of the whole of human experience" (Perez 152).

Banks asserts that one way to address diverse cultures in a classroom is to select readings that reflect student population. This way, students will see their images in the curriculum (466). Classroom attrition often results from instructors not acknowledging cultural differences. There are "wide discrepancies in the academic achievement of groups as Blacks and mainstream White youths, between Mexican American and Japanese American students" (452). To retain students

> [t]eachers should recognize that students bring a variety of learning, cognitive, and motivational styles to the classroom, and that while certain characteristics are associated with specific ethnic and social-class groups, these characteristics are distributed throughout the total student population. This means that the teacher should use a variety of teaching styles and content that will appeal to diverse students. (466)

To emphasize the influence culture has on learning style, Oxford and Anderson conducted studies on African-American, Greek-American, Chinese-American, Mexican-American, Hawaiian-American, Navajo-American, and Anglo-Saxon-American students. The researchers found eight different learning styles, most of which can be traced to cultural behavioral preferences. If teachers understand these cultural differences, they can adjust their teaching style to reach students of various cultures in their classes (201-215). "[M]any Native American students do not respond verbally in class, nor do they make direct eye contact, as both behaviors are considered impolite in their culture" (Henderson 52). Native Americans value and develop clear-sightedness and "skills in the use of imagery, perceive globally, have reflective thinking patterns [. . .] schools [. . .] should provide quiet times for thinking, and emphasize visual stimuli " (Guild 17). If a teacher expects these students to react assertively, as many European cultures do, the Native American student will fail because their cultural learning behavior will not permit it (Henderson 47-55).

> Don't expect to see Native [Eskimo Yup'ik] students [in university classrooms] shooting their hands up in the air with the "I know, I know" look. And don't think less of them for not doing so. It is not our way. Our culture teaches modesty. For us success means not to stand out from the crowd but to live in harmony with everything around us. (Barnhardt 116)

"Schools in the United States orient their curricula to the analytical style, but black people and lower-income people tend to use a predominately relational style" (Claxton and Murrel qtd. in Purkiss 92). Black students value oral occurrences, physical activities, and loyalty in relationships (Guild 17). Not addressing the student's learning style may result in the student dropping courses or withdrawing from school (Henderson 47-55).

Further, Miville, Koonce, Darlington, and Whitlock researched the relationship between racial/cultural identity and ego identity among African Americans and Mexican Americans. They found "ego identity was significantly related to racial identity for African Americans and cultural identity for Mexican Americans" (208). Moreover, they found that "both African Americans and Mexican Americans have developed [. . .] identities based on their respective group's history of exposure to widespread and continuing discrimination" (216). Results showed that for both groups to achieve ego identity, or a positive sense of self, they had to achieve a positive racial or cultural identity. African Americans' "ego identity [. . .] linked a naive racial worldview and a conforming racial identity" (217). However, Mexican American "ego identity [. . .] linked with cultural identity [. . .] but less so for African Americans" (217). Thus, "both African Americans and Mexican Americans self-reported race-ethnicity as an Important or very Important Identity area, [. . .] whereas White American participants rated this area as least Important" (209). A successful teacher wants to take all of these ethnic elements into consideration in the classroom.

In his book, Bootstraps: From an American Academic of Color, Victor Villanueva describes his personal experiences with public school teachers and university professors. Today, he is Victor Villanueva, university professor, but there was a time that he was a "would-be dropout" (8). Throughout his book, he describes many negative experiences with teachers at all academic levels and concludes that "[c]olor isn't always race when it comes to teachers. It's attitude, more an understanding of where we live than where we're from" (2). Villanueva describes a teacher that he calls Mr. D.

> Mr. D could speak *with* us. To speak of Julius Caesar was to speak of how fighting, ganging up, was seen as a solution for many people over a long time. But the power really depended on knowing how to use language, the language of Mark Antony, for instance. Mr. D provided the spark that would flare again some thirteen years later. (3)

Villanueva says that Mr. D understands where his students came from; he understands their culture (3).

In a study performed by Texas Tech University, cultural norms for Mexican-Americans decree conformity to value family and social relationships that conform culturally, and relate with "generalities and patterns" (Guild 17, Rivas 67). The traditional Mexican-American family structure is

> paternalistic, authoritarian, and extended-family oriented. It has also been viewed as having strong and clear separation of sex roles, strong loyalty and respect for parents and older adults, and strict child-rearing practices. The cultural values that are expressed through the Mexican-American socialization practices include: (1) identification with family, community, and ethnic group, (2) strict status and role definition of family, and (3) personalization of interpersonal relationships. (Rivas 68-69)

This may be why Mexican-American students many times develop friendships with their teachers "and are more comfortable with broad concepts than component facts and specifics" (Guild 17). Although the Texas Tech University study did not find the traditional cognitive difference between the Mexican-American subjects and the Anglo-American subjects, the researcher reveals that it was performed in an urban setting, in the Texas Panhandle far (approximately 1500 miles) from the Mexican border in the Lower Rio Grande Valley, and the parents of the subjects are Spanish-English bilingual (Rivas 71, 74). The same study performed at the University might produce different results because most of the students come from the surrounding agricultural area, the university is 15 miles from the Mexican-American border, and many of the parents of the students are monolingual Spanish.

From a curricular perspective, cultural diversity can be achieved by integrating literature from various cultures by including authors representative of those cultures. "[T]he college [. . .] [should have] specific classes that reflect an interest in cultural diversity, including 'African American History,' 'Chicano History,' and some classes in the area of women's studies" (Purkiss 92).

Many teachers are not trained to teach writing and, therefore, are at a loss when a student is able to speak well, but is not able to write well. Speaking and writing are the major functions of language which creates a strange relationship between them. Some strategies of oral language, as expression, exists in written language, but not all oral strategies can be transferred to the writing process. Many times the non-standard pronunciation and word use of an ethnic group can interfere with standard writing production. One strategy for improving the teaching of writing is to use the oral-literacy approach by taking advantage of cultures with an oral literacy and show the relationship to writing. Another strategy is to use color of expression to motivate writing by allowing students to emphasize their cultural differences. With foreign students, a good strategy is the audio-lingual approach which is training the ear to hearing correct language, then transferring that skill to producing standard writing. A good back up strategy is to send students for additional tutoring at the Writing Center. The whole idea is to recognize the correlation between oral and written language (Sterling 15-20).

The United States contains many cultures that do not stem from foreign countries. These cultures all have their own vernacular, just "as Chicano English,

Puerto Rican English, Vietnamese English or Navajo English" (Hagemann 75). Some are rural, with each area having its own (such as Appalachian English and rural African American), and some are urban poor working class; however, each language system has its own dialect, accent, and intonation and rhythms. When students from these backgrounds come to college, they have big hopes, but they know they speak a different kind of English than colleges accept. They do not speak Standard English. However, many students have "a native's intuitive sense of what's grammatical in his home language" (75). As a result, they are poor readers of English, and their "essays sound very oral, and pay little attention to punctuation" or grammar (75). Students tend to emphasize the oral side of learning as lectures and study groups. Perhaps teachers would want to do as McAndrew and Hurlbert suggest and allow students to spell according to their phonetic sensibilities while the teacher focuses on more important errors. This would take the pressure off students to perform while learning to correct their more serious errors (5-7).

> [F]or working class, language minority students who typically speak various Englishes that are considered nonstandard, the transition [from home to college] is much more difficult. The rules of their home discourses don't overlap as much [as those from middle class English literate homes] with those of the academic world. As a result, many language minority students struggle with the rules and conventions of speaking and writing "school talk." (Hagemann 75)

Reising and Hils state that most college and university students generally come from urban areas that are very different from rural students who probably have not been exposed to a live symphony, a professional play, a rock concert, a large library, a large book store, or eaten exotic food that comes from outside their region. "Their intellectual and cultural world is essentially that of their fundamentalist religious beliefs. To top it all, they are probably self-deprecating or even have a sense of inferiority in the face of mainstream national culture" (4).

Instead of understanding and embracing the positive elements that these students bring to the classroom, teachers seem to focus on their so called weaknesses, "rural students commonly receive indictments such as 'unteachable,' 'indifferent,' and 'They can't write, think or appreciate.' The best they can hope for is sympathy throughout the semester and a D (for disadvantaged) at the end of it" (4). Reising and Hils "maintain also, that it is the comp teachers, rather than the students themselves, who are too often disadvantaged by urban biases and popular distortions of rural life" (4).

> Mina Shaughnessy argues that students have trouble precisely with academic writing, which 'serves a different purpose from speech' and 'tends to exploit syntactic possibilities that speech either need not or cannot exploit.' From Shaughnessy's perspective, it is the students themselves rather than their teachers who feel the difference the strongest. (qtd. in Killingsworth 28)

As Guild stated, these students have a daily cultural adjustment to the culture of the school and its teachers (19). Despite this, these students need

> a curriculum that prepares them for the literacy practices of the academy. They need to learn, for example, to be critical readers and writers, to state claims they can support persuasively, to deal with conflicting points of view in texts, and to re-present those ideas in texts to achieve their own purposes. But they also need what middle class students already have: access to formal, written, standard American English, to supplement their home discourses. They need a detailed awareness of how home discourse is similar to and different from Standard American English and an ability to shift smoothly from their home discourse to academic English whenever they want or need to. (Hagemann 75)

In most college courses, students are asked to give their perceptions of teacher classroom performance. Levy, et al, researched the influence of culture on students' perceptions of teacher effectiveness. They found that classes with a large number of non-Anglo-Americans students perceived the Anglo-American teacher as dominating (29). Also, Latin American students who speak Spanish at home were more likely than other groups to believe this. Moreover, the more different ethnicities in a class, the greater perception of teacher dominance. However, a class filled with Anglo-Americans perceived the teacher as less dominant (48). An understanding that a teacher's interpersonal behavior can create a positive classroom atmosphere is vitally important to the quality of teaching (29).

Students from developing countries as India and the Phillippines have different problems. Their countries have been successful in educating quantitatively, but not qualitatively. A study showed that the students were learning to read focusing on surface strategies, instead of reading for meaning, as theme and main ideas. Therefore, educators in these countries looked to Western countries to improve their educational system. They found that in Western countries such as Sweden, Great Britain, and Australia, the approaches to deep and surface learning are comparable. Watkins found for the first time cross-cultural validity of Western factors influenced student learning. Nevertheless, the Eastern countries still feared Western social science theories and measuring systems being imposed on them (165-190).

Research by Zhang and Sternberg give evidence that thinking styles may vary from culture to culture. The researchers describe thinking styles as "a preferred way of thinking or of doing things. A style is not an ability, but rather a preference in the use of the abilities one has" (198). The researchers studied high school and university students in Hong Kong, mainland China, and the United States. They found

> First, thinking styles contributed to academic achievement above self-rated abilities. Second, thinking styles are closely related to students' learning approaches. Third, thinking styles have significant relationships with students' characteristics, including age, birth order, gender

socioeconomic status, number of hobbies, leadership experience, and working and traveling experience. Fourth, thinking styles are statistically related to self-esteem. (198)

Summary/Conclusion

Without intending to, educators silence minority students by using the Initiation-Response-Evaluation (IRE) teaching behavioral style. Mainstream middle class students respond best to IRE because most are of European American heritage whose families use this teaching style in the home.

Teachers need to be aware that learning styles differ from culture to culture, gender to gender, and within ethnic categories, for example: Native American and Eskimo tribes, various European and Latin American countries. However, as individuals become Americanized, they tend to evolve from the learning style of their country of origin while maintaining a connection to their culture.

Cultural identity can, or cannot, be the same as racial identity because there can be several races within an ethnicity or culture. Educators will want to appeal to the diversity between and within cultures. In that regard, I agree with Zhang and Sternberg's implications for teachers.

The first implication of Zhang and Sternberg's study for teachers is: (1) the reason some students do not perform well in school may be a mismatch between students' thinking styles and the learning style preferred by the teacher, (2) teachers need to be aware of the thinking style preferred by the predominate culture of the students and the teacher's preferred style, (3) teachers need to be well educated about thinking styles of both gender and cross-cultural differences. When teachers are aware of these types of differences between students, they can better adapt their teaching styles to include all students (211).

The second implication for teachers, thinking styles with learning styles, is they could use the relationship between thinking styles and learning by allowing students to give their own opinions on the subjects they learn. Further, students could choose their own subjects and/or special projects. This could give opportunities for students to think for themselves and to work on their favorite projects. When students do this, they will inevitably "take a deep approach to learning and employ thinking styles that will allow them to think more creatively and come up with norm-challenging ideas" (Zhang and Sternberg 215).

The third implication of Zhang and Sternberg study is for teachers regarding thinking styles with student characteristics, including the Chinese and English versions, showed the relationship between certain thinking styles and various student characteristics including age, birth order, sex, college major, subject area taught, college class level, socioeconomic status, and traveling and working experiences. The findings supported the contention that styles are socialized, and, therefore, with the proper learning environment, students may modify their thinking styles. This can be done by teachers lecturing, facilitating group discussion and activities, and using cooperative learning so that all students can benefit. Teachers could use various evaluation methods, such as multiple-choice test, short essays, individual projects, and group projects so that all students can succeed. Further, teachers could encourage students to achieve an understanding of different thinking styles so that students could become more aware of how they are using their abilities. Also, teachers could improve teaching and learning by using students' daily life experiences and oral heritage for educational purpose, and promote creative thinking (Zhang and Sternberg 219).

Zhang and Sternberg's fourth research point provided "[t]he major value of this study is that it empirically verified the relationship between thinking styles and one of the important affective domains, that is, self-esteem. This verification supported the argument that thinking styles should be related to personality" (Zhang and Sternberg 220). This means that students with high self-esteem would also be more self-confident about whatever they do. "This self-confidence leads them to be self-instructed and self-directed (legislative style), and to perform their tasks in a nontraditional way (liberal style). Students with higher self-esteem also would be comfortable with what they do to the extent that they prioritize their tasks (hierarchical style)" (220). Teachers could use the relationship of thinking styles with self-esteem by giving students the opportunity to succeed academically and experientially. When students feel self-confident, they may think creatively when doing assignments. It is essential that teachers use various teaching methods allowing for a variety of thinking and learning styles (220-21).

Losey also refers to the "cultural mismatch theory" (11) and argues that the primary reason for it is the teaching style that favors the mainstream, middle-class home student because the Initiation-Response-Evaluation (IRE) is used in the home as well as in the classroom. When a student interprets the classroom climate and deduces that she is at a distinct disadvantage, the situation effectively silences her and she will refuse to speak out and/or join in classroom discussion. This is especially true of those who do not speak generally accepted standard English, especially those among "working class Anglo and rural black families, Native Americans, ethnic Hawaiians, inner city black youths, and [. . .] bilingual Chicanos" (10). Teachers need to make the classroom less threatening and in effect level the playing field for all ethnicities.

Chapter 3. Methodology: Data Collection

Introduction

    The purpose of this study is to gain insights as to why there is a history of a high rate of students repeating First-Year Composition because they did not pass the course with a C or better or because they dropped the course mid-semester. The prevailing perception within the University English Department is that students whose first language is Spanish, not English, do not succeed in First-Year Composition during their first enrollment because of poor reading and writing skills in English. "In fact, one of the most common strategies for dealing with these students, flunking them, is also the least effective" (Perez 151). First, with my dissertation committee, I developed the questions for a survey and follow-up interview to be administered to students currently enrolled in First-Year Composition and to faculty currently teaching First-Year Composition. Then in order to attain permission to begin my research, I first had to gain permission from both Indiana University of Pennsylvania's and the University's Institutional Review Board for the Protection of Human Subjects In Research Committees. Upon receiving approval from both schools' committees, I proceeded to administer the Student Survey by placing memos in the mailboxes of all teachers currently teaching this course asking for permission to visit their classroom to ask their students to participate in the study.

    Although done without a pilot study, I believe the responses of both students and faculty are reliable and valid because some of the replies were belligerent, accusative, but they seemed honest. Then I solicited faculty volunteers by placing a memo in the mailboxes of faculty currently teaching First-Year Composition. After the students in the classes of the faculty who volunteered and the faculty also completed a separate survey, I contacted by telephone those students and faculty, who gave me permission to interview them by signing a form attached to the survey. Many of those that I was able to talk to, made an appointment with me to audio-tape an interview with them.

Surveys

Upon receiving approval from both schools' committees, I proceeded to administer the Student Survey by placing memos in the mailboxes of all teachers currently teaching this course asking for permission to visit their classroom to ask their students to participate in the study. Of the 21 teachers who received the memo, eight gave permission allowing the researcher to visit their classrooms. In the classroom, the instructor was asked to leave so the students would feel little to no intimidation and would answer more freely and honestly.

Once alone with the students, I explained that I am a doctoral student at Indiana University of Pennsylvania (IUP) and conducting research for my dissertation through the IUP Graduate English Department. The purpose of this research study is to gain insights on the teaching styles of teachers of composition courses and the learning styles of students enrolled in composition courses. Further, I stressed that participation in this study was voluntary. There were no risks to the student for taking part in this research. Any information obtained during this study which could identify students will be kept strictly confidential and destroyed as soon as this dissertation is accepted by the IUP Graduate school. No one will be personally identified and participation will have no bearing on anyone's academic standing or on services received from the college or community agencies. All questionnaire responses will be considered only in combination with that from other participants. The survey contains a total of twenty questions: the first ten questions are answered by filling in a bubble on a Scantron, and the second ten are short answer questions. Many questions were not answered because the 282 participating students were told not to answer questions that made them feel uncomfortable; therefore, the total number of respondents to the first ten questions may not add up to the total of 282 answers.

Also, I asked those eight teachers who allowed me to survey their students If they would complete a Faculty Survey, and six did. As with the students, I explained that participation in this study was voluntary and the purpose of this research study was to gain insights on the teaching styles of teachers of composition courses and the learning styles of students enrolled in composition courses. Further, I stressed that there were no risks for taking part in this research. Any information obtained during this study which could identify anyone would be kept strictly confidential and destroyed as soon as this dissertation is accepted by the IUP Graduate school. All questionnaire responses will be considered only in combination with that from other participants. The faculty questionnaire consisted of fifteen short answer questions which the faculty members completed in the privacy of their office and returned to me.

Teaching Style

One of the areas researched by my survey is teaching style which Dunn and Frazier maintain is a behavior, rather than a methodology (347-367). Behavior, in this sense, predicts the type of teaching strategies or methods that a teacher uses to conduct her class. Erickson and Erickson argue that an instructor, to develop an effective teaching style, should develop certain skills that arouse interest by providing introductions; provide organization with examples, anecdotes, or illustrations to explain and clarify the subject; ask questions; use a variety of materials and methods; communicate respect and concern for students; use valid and reliable examinations; and give feedback which allows students to know where they stand (58).

When teachers adapt their teaching style to meet the needs of their class, learning and understanding increase (Davidson 36-38). The above research made me question if students perceive that instructors use an effective teaching style. Therefore, I created the following questions in the Student Survey:

Student Survey Questions

1   I like it when a teacher talks or lectures about new material as a class, rather than in small groups.

9   I prefer a teacher who conducts a relaxed classroom.

10   I prefer a teacher who conducts a strictly controlled classroom.

11   Without mentioning names (just say third grade teacher, etc.), which of all of your teachers did you like best? Why did you like this teacher best?

12   Without mentioning names (just say third grade teacher, etc.), which of all of your teachers did you like least? Why did you like this teacher least?

13   What does a good teacher do while teaching?

14   What does a poor teacher do while teaching?

17   What does an English teacher do to make an English class a good class?

18   What does an English teacher do to make an English class a boring class?

Faculty Survey Questions

Likewise, I wanted to learn what the faculty perceives as good teaching style and if they perceive they connect with the student's learning style; ergo, I composed of the following questions in the Faculty Survey:

1   Describe how you teach writing in your classes.

7   Describe what you think good teaching is.

8   What are the goals for your Composition class?

9   Why do you want your students to learn to write correct English?

10   What are your hopes and aspirations for your students?

15   Do you like to teach Composition? Explain the reason for your answer.

Faculty Interview Questions

1   How do you explain what an essay is to students?

2   How do you explain the process of writing to students?

3   What do you look for in student writing?

4   What do you consider good writing?

7   Do you group students to read each other's essays and give feedback?

8	When grading essays, what errors do you mark?
9	Do you write end notes on essays? Why or why not?
10	If you write notes, what do you write in them?

Learning Style

Another area of my study is learning styles which are the "unique ways whereby an individual gathers and processes information and are the means by which an individual prefers to learn" (Davidson 36). Because culture is the basis of learning styles, learning occurs through the sensory channels or pathways which students use their perception, memory and all of their senses to give, receive, and store information. Culture will influence an individual's approach to learning, so the strength of these traits and race are not related, and generalizations cannot be made (Reiff 17, 18). Cultures have distinct learning patterns, "but the great variation among individuals within groups means that educators must use diverse teaching strategies with all students" (Guild 16).

The above research led me to the development of the following questions:

Student Survey Questions

4	I like it when the teacher asks the students to work on in-class projects in small groups.
5	I like to try to work on projects alone, rather than in small groups.
6	I prefer to work alone when trying to figure out how to do an assignment.
7	I prefer to work with others when trying to figure out how to do an assignment.
15	What does a good student do when learning new material?
16	What does a poor student do when learning new material?

Faculty Survey Questions

3	What learning problems do your students face?
14	What problems do you encounter in teaching Composition?

Faculty Interview Questions

5   How do you deal with students who have difficulty in grasping academic writing?

6   How do you encourage class participation?

From these questions, I wanted to learn if the students felt a bond and support from their teacher, for without that connection, learning does not happen as well.

Cultural Identity

The third area researched in my study is the effect of culture on learning. The usual student population of a classroom in the Lower Rio Grande Valley of Texas is almost totally Hispanic students with a few Caucasian pupils and other nationalities. However, within the Hispanic group, there are various nationalities that represent different cultures. In the Valley, there is also a large Asian population consisting of various nationalities. Further, several Middle Eastern, African, as well as other European nationalities have representation in the general population.

A student's culture often features in a student's learning style. Many academics fail to associate a student's performance levels with their cultural background, and cultural learning styles (Kolodny par. 1-6). Cho and Forde conducted a study that included students from the White, Hispanic, Asian/Pacific Islander, African-American, Native American, and other ethnic groups and found significant differences in the learning styles of the White group and all other ethnic groups. There were also significant differences between the students based on socio-economic status (86-95). The various cultures have different values. The mainstream White American value "independence, analytic thinking, objectivity, and accuracy. These values translate into learning experiences that focus on competition, information, tests and grades, and linear logic. These patterns are prevalent in most American schools" (Guild 17-18). With a classroom of almost totally Hispanic students, there are myriad of cultural differences within that group that can aid the teacher in selecting teaching styles.

However, the problem may not lie with teaching or learning styles, but Raul Ybarra found that the problems stemmed from a student's cultural identity. He discovered that students could perform poorly in school because they feel alienated from their heritage for personal reasons which becomes acerbated when they cannot identify with her "Anglo–mainstream instructors" (161). Moreover, students may have been taught by teachers in her country that the only valid opinion was the instructor's, and therefore, students have no right to voice opinions. Further, students in these countries may have "equated speaking out in class with getting punished" (164).

Many Hispanics and other minority students become frustrated, angry, suspicious, and mistrust school systems. The instructor must not only hear what their students tell them, but really listen to them. Ortiz and Garcia wrote, "When teachers fail to recognize the cultural differences among learning styles, students react in negative ways to the instruction" (qtd. in Oxford and Anderson 201). Many students believe that something is wrong with them when they cannot please instructors, so they feel their only option is to drop the class, or to drop out of school, although not all students do.

This research led to the development of the following culture related questions:

Student Survey Questions

19   Do you think Hispanic teachers make good role models? Why or why not?

20   What does your family think about your attending college?

Faculty Survey Questions

2   How would you describe the students in your class?

4   What kind of student has been your best student?

5   What kind of student has been your worst student?

6   Do you use the work of Hispanic authors in your course? If you use Hispanic authors, which authors do you use?

11   What do you like best about living in the Rio Grande Valley?

12   What do like least about living in the Rio Grande Valley?

13   Do you incorporate the student's oral family history in your classes? If you do, why do you do this; if not, why don't you do this?

Victor Villanueva asserts "[c]olor isn't always race when it comes to teachers. It's attitude, more an understanding of where we live than where we're from" (2). Villanueva states that "Mr. D could speak *with* us" (3). Because Mr. D understands where his students came from; he understands their culture (3). Villanueva's last two sentences made me wonder if these students perceive that the instructor understands them and speaks *with* them, and caused me to develop the following questions:

Student Survey Additional Questions

2   I feel uncomfortable when the teacher tells the class to interrupt the lecture when we do not understand something or have a question.

3   I like it when the teacher asks the students to speak out in class.

8   I prefer a teacher with whom I can disagree and who does not get upset, but will talk out the misunderstanding with me.

Since the research showed that there can be a misunderstanding of learning styles based on culture, I wanted to learn if the students felt culturally safe with their teacher and that instructor's teaching style.

Interviews

Using the same research, I developed two sets of ten questions. One was used in the student interviews and the other in the instructor interviews. Students find it difficult to evaluate their own learning style, so I did not ask them to do so. But they can more easily evaluate an instructor's teaching style, therefore, all of the student interview questions ask about teaching style. Also, most of the instructor questions focus on teaching style.

Teaching Styles

Student Questions

1 In all the English classes that you have taken, what did your favorite teacher do that you liked best?
2 In all the English classes that you have taken, what did your favorite teacher do that you liked worst?
3 What teaching technique that the English teacher used helped you the most?
4 What teaching technique that the English teacher used helped you the least?
5 Do you like it when teachers put you in a group of 3 or 4 students and you read and give feedback on each other's essays?
6 What could the teacher do to encourage more class participation?
7 What do teachers do to discourage students?
8 When teachers write comments on your essays, what do you like least?
9 When teachers write comments on your essays, what do you like most?
10 Do you like it when teachers write a special note on your essays?

Faculty Questions

1 How do you explain what an essay is to students?
2 How do you explain the process of writing to students?
3 What do you look for in student writing?
4 What do you consider good writing?
7 Do you group students to read each other's essays and give feedback?
8 When grading essays, what errors do you mark?
9 Do you write end notes on essays? Why or why not?
10 If you write notes, what do you write in them?

From the responses to the above questions, I looked to discover if students and teachers felt connected to each other. Without that bond there can be little true communication and little learning occurring.

Learning Styles
Faculty Questions

These two Instructor Interview questions focused on the instructors perception of student's learning styles.

5   How do you deal with students who have difficulty in grasping academic writing?

6   How do you encourage class participation?

I wanted to know if teachers were truly aware of student learning style. Are instructors really sensitive to different learning styles and to cultural differences which determine if pupils speak out in class or not and find another way for students to participate in class.

Interview Procedures
Students

Most of the 37 student interviews were conducted in a private room in the University Library and in my faculty office. The students were asked to sign a separate Informed Consent Form for the personal interview. I reminded the students that the interview would be audio taped, all answers would be used in a group with no individual identification. Further, the questions focused on aspects of teaching that assist learning academic writing. I added that I wanted to learn which teaching methods do not help their learning and how teachers interact both with the students, and with the course content. Further, I asked students what the teacher could have done to encourage more class participation, and what would they have liked to see the teacher do. Also, I wanted to know about teacher comments written on essays and other homework. All of the students agreed to give me the requested information.

Faculty

All of the six teachers were interviewed in their faculty office. Each was asked to sign a separate Informed Consent Form for the personal interview. I reminded each teacher that the interview would be audio taped, the questions would be nonthreatening and I let them see the questions before the interview began. The teachers were asked how they approach teaching essay writing, how they demonstrate the process of writing, and how they deal with the variety of learning styles. Also, they were asked how they evaluate good writing, how they mark essays, and if they write notes to the students on the essays, and what they write in the note.

From these questions I analyzed student and faculty perceptions of the teaching styles currently used in English 1301 First-Year Composition, the learning styles of students currently enrolled in the course, and the relationship of the Hispanic culture to teaching and learning styles.

Chapter 4. Analysis of the Data

Student Surveys

Of the 282 students who completed the survey, 118 were male and 159 were female. Most (224) were first-year students, 43 were sophomores, seven juniors, two seniors, and six were high school students enrolled in a college course. Sixty-five percent, or 183 students were repeating the course. Because the Registrar stated that he could not provide me with specific data regarding a particular student, I have no way of knowing if any of the participating students fall into the following data. The UTPA IRB (Institutional Review Board for the Protection of Human Subjects) committee did not allow me to ask students if they failed or had to repeat First-Year Composition because they felt that it would make participants uncomfortable. I stated that students would be told not to respond to any question that made them feel uncomfortable, but the committee pointed out that my statistics would be skewed. I did not ask the question; however, according to English Department records, a total of 268 (22.1%) students did not pass First-Year Composition with a C or better that semester. Also, 25 (02.1%) students withdrew from the University, and 143 (11.8%) dropped the course.

The survey contains a total of twenty questions: the first ten questions are answered by filling in a bubble on a Scantron, and the second ten are short answer questions. Students were told not to answer questions that made them feel uncomfortable; therefore, because of the unanswered questions, the total number of respondents to the first ten questions may not add up to the total of 282 respondents.

Respondents were asked to answer the questions on the Scantron by placing a mark next to the letter that best describes their response: (A) Strongly agree, (B) Agree, (C) Undecided, (D) Disagree, (E) Strongly Disagree.
See Appendix A for a copy of the student Informed Consent Form and Student Survey.

Analysis

The following questions focused on preferred teaching techniques that met preferred learning styles.

Question one stated "I like it when a teacher talks or lectures about new material as a class, rather than in small groups." Most of the respondents 228 or 81% agreed (117 said they strongly agreed, while 111 said they agreed). A total of 38 students or 13.5% disagreed (34 disagreed and four strongly disagreed). Fifteen were undecided. One question was left blank.

Question four stated, "I like it when the teacher asks the students to work on class projects in small groups." Seventy-five percent (213 or 75.55%) agreed. (Ninety-six agreed, and 117 strongly agreed). Thirty-nine or 14% disagreed; (29 disagreed and ten strongly disagreed). Twenty-nine were undecided. One was left blank.

The fifth question asked, "I like to try to work on projects alone, rather than in small groups." A large number of respondents (94 or 33.5%) were undecided. However, a total of 108 or 38.5% agreed (55 agreeing and 53 strongly agreed). Further, 43 or 15.25% disagreed (42 disagreeing, and one strongly disagreeing). Thirty-seven or 13% did not answer the question.

Question six stated, "I prefer to work alone when trying to figure out how to do an assignment." A majority of 155 or 55% disagreed. (One-hundred-six disagreed and 49 strongly disagreed). Eighty-two or 29.25% agreed (48 agreeing and 34 strongly agreeing). Forty-four were undecided. One was left blank.

The seventh question asked, "I prefer to work with others when trying to figure out how to do an assignment." Most students (197 or 70%) agreed (102 agreed, and 95 strongly agreed). But 53 or 19% disagreed (46 disagreeing and seven strongly disagreeing). Thirty-two were undecided.

Because most of The University's student population are recent immigrant or are first or second generation Mexican Americans, it is understandable why most preferred small groups. According to Jimenez, most minorities and recent immigrants are Field Dependent learners which means they work well in groups; first grasp the big picture, then the specific project; are motivated by group work, group competition, and group achievement. Further they are more affected by distracting noise and movement when trying to solve a problem or work on a project (Jimenez 17). As they become assimilated into the American culture, they develop into Field Independent learners, which Anglo-Americans tend to prefer because they can work well alone, can see the specific problem to work on and its relationship to the whole. Also, they become more competitive, and analytical.

With a classroom of almost totally Hispanic students, there are myriad of cultural differences within that group that can aid the teacher in selecting teaching styles. The next questions focused on cultural classroom behavior.

The second question asked if students feel uncomfortable when the teacher tells the class to interrupt the lecture when they do not understand something or have a question. A majority (148 or 52.5%) of the students disagreed. (Seventy-nine students disagreed, and 69 strongly disagreed). However, a little over a third of the respondents (109 or 38.75%) agreed (52 agreed, and 57 strongly agreed). Twenty-four were undecided. One survey was left blank,

The third question asked "I like it when the teacher asks the students to speak out in class." Two-thirds (193 or 68..5%) stated that they agreed. (Ninety-one said they agreed, but 102 strongly agreed). Only 51 or 18.5% disagreed; (41 disagreed and 10 strongly disagreed). Thirty-eight were undecided.

The students who marked that they do not feel comfortable interrupting the teacher may come from cultures that do not permit this behavior. Henderson pointed out that the culture of many Native American students requires that they do not respond verbally in class, nor do they make direct eye contact, as both behaviors are considered impolite (52). Also, Native Americans value and develop clear-sightedness and "skills in the use of imagery, perceive globally, have reflective thinking patterns [. . .] schools [. . .] should provide quiet times for thinking, and emphasize visual stimuli " (Guild 17). These students cannot live up to a teacher's expectations of reacting assertively because the Native American student cannot and will not go against their cultural learning behavior (Henderson 47-55). "Schools in the United States orient their curricula to the analytical style, but black people and lower-income people tend to use a predominately relational style" (Claxton and Murrel qtd. in Purkiss 92). Black students value oral exchanges, physical activities, and loyalty in relationships (Guild 17).

Teaching the Initiation-Response-Evaluation (IRE) favors the mainstream, middle-class home student and creates what Losey refers to as the "cultural mismatch theory" because IRE is used in the home as well as in the classroom (11). When a student believes that she is at a disadvantage, she becomes silent and will refuse to speak or join in classroom discussion. Those most prone to behave in this manner are those who do not speak generally accepted standard English, especially those among "working class Anglo and rural black families, Native Americans, ethnic Hawaiians, inner city black youths, and [. . .] bilingual Chicanos" (10).

Raul Ybarra argues that the participation problem may stem from a student's cultural identity. If students have a cultural identification problem, it may cause them classroom participation problems. Many times there is no identification problem but a cultural one. Some cultures effectively silence students so she feels she had no right to voice her opinions because teachers had convinced her that the only valid opinion was the instructor's and she "equated speaking out in class with getting punished" (164).

The next group of questions looked at the type of teacher the students prefer.

Question eight, "I prefer a teacher with whom I can disagree and who does not get upset, but will talk out the misunderstanding with me." Two-hundred sixty-one or 92.75% agreed (76 agreeing and 185 strongly agreeing). Only five disagreed, none strongly disagreed, and sixteen were undecided.

When students feel free to voice their point of view without teacher censorship then students will be more willing to join in class discussion.

Levy, et al, researched the influence of culture on students' perceptions of teacher effectiveness. They found that classes with a large number of non-Anglo-Americans perceived the teacher as dominating (29). Also, Latin American students who speak Spanish at home were more likely than other groups to believe this. Moreover, the more different ethnicities in a class, the greater perception of teacher dominance. However, a class filled with Anglo-Americans perceived the teacher as less dominant (48). An understanding that a teacher's interpersonal behavior can create a positive classroom atmosphere is vitally important to the quality of teaching (29).

The ninth question asked, "I prefer a teacher who conducts a relaxed classroom." Most agreed (256 or 89.5%) (88 agreeing and 168 strongly agreeing). A total of ten disagreed (six disagreeing and four strongly disagreeing). Fifteen were undecided. One was left blank.

The tenth question was, "I prefer a teacher who conducts a strictly controlled classroom." A total of 177 or 62.7% disagreed (100 disagreeing and 77 strongly disagreeing). Forty-five or 16% agreed (30 agreeing and 15 strongly agreeing). Fifty-six were undecided and four did not answer the question and left it blank

Most of the students agreed that they preferred a relaxed classroom. "When the classroom feels comfortable enough for each person to relax, then students from various backgrounds can take the risk of expressing their views, resulting in a richer blend of perspectives" (Hughes, Romeo, and Romeo 411).

The next ten questions asked the student to give a short answer to a question. Spelling and grammar are not corrected. The students were to give in their own words their opinions of what makes a good or poor teacher, good teaching style, and to tell by their answers what their preferred learning style is.

Question: 11 asked "Without mentioning names (just say third grade teacher, etc.), which of all of your teachers did you like best? Why did you like this teacher best?" The quoted statements below are a selected representation of all the responses on the surveys.

He taught in a way we understood he used our language rather than being proper all the time.

It was a very relaxed environment yet he had control of the class and his lectures were almost like conversation he had with the class.

Challenged me and treated us as learning human beings, not another herd of students.

He can relate to our backgrounds.

He not only taught us but learned with us as a friend.

The concept of a teacher in Mexico is very different from the role of a teacher in the United states. Mexican-American students often times develop friendships with their teachers and prefer that instructors act as coach (Guild 17). American teachers often dominate the classroom and act as judge of both behavior and class work.

Culture influences students' perceptions of teacher effectiveness and domination when in classes with a large number of non-Anglo-Americans (Levy, et al 29). More often, students who speak Spanish at home were more likely than other groups to believe this. In addition, when there are many different ethnicities in a class, the greater perception of teacher dominance. However, a class filled with Anglo-Americans perceived the same teacher as less dominant (48). A teacher's understanding that her interpersonal behavior can create a positive classroom atmosphere is vitally important to the quality of teaching (29). When teaching Mexican-American students, It is important to understand that many times they develop friendships with their teachers (Guild 17).

Question: 12 asked "Which of all of your teachers did you like least? (Name not necessary, just say third grade teacher, etc.) Why did you like this teacher the least?" The quoted statements below are a selected representation of all the responses on the surveys.

My past [English]1301 professors in 13 grade. Probably because I'm a ESL student and I wasn't able to confront them just did my work and if it was bad, I just leave it like that.

Maybe it was my recent English teacher because she never admits she's wrong and when in a discussion she always had the last word.

Pre-calculus teacher: she talks straight from the book. The examples are from the book. I could also teach the class straight from the book.

My 11th grade math teacher. She was very rude and wouldn't give help to students. She would also put me down when I asked questions and said I didn't belong in her class.

One teacher I had last semester in my [English] 1301. I dropped the course because she did not explain anything and she was kind of racist about Mexicans.

What some students may describe as poor teaching, rudeness, and lack of respect by the teacher could actually be what Losey refers to as "cultural mismatch theory" (11). Losey asserts that when the heritage of the teacher and the majority of the students in her class do not match, the students may not be able to fulfill the expectations and may "misread" the behavior of the teacher. This creates mis-communication for both the students and the teacher.

Zhang and Sternberg found that when teachers are aware of differences between students, they can better adapt their teaching styles to include all students. There may be a mismatch between students' thinking styles and the learning style preferred by the teacher, so teachers will want to be aware of the cultures of her students and the thinking style preferred by the that culture. Further, teachers should know about thinking styles of both genders and cross-cultural differences (211).

Cultural identity is one of the reasons students fear classroom participation problems. Raul Ybarra found that some cultures do not give students the right to voice their opinions, and when they do they often equate speaking in class with punishment (164). It is not unusual for Hispanic and other minority students to become frustrated, angry, suspicious, and mistrust school systems. When they cannot please instructors, students believe that something is wrong with them, so they drop the class, or withdraw from school. To prevent this, teachers need to understand who their students are, where they come from, and their culture (Ybarra 168).

Question: 13 asked "What does a good teacher do while teaching?"

The quoted statements below are a selected representation of all the responses on the surveys.

Addresses the class while teaching and ask for feedback. Wants the students to pitch in and feel comfortable doing it. It's so much easier to learn that way.

A good teacher is friendly and wants us to learn no matter what. She will always be willing to meet with us in one-in-one.

Respect every student no matter the level of knowledge that the student may have. Try to make you understand and if you don't understand, takes time to explain again until you get it. Also someone who has time after class for any other problems or questions.

Makes the students laugh, a little good humor involved in the lecture has always helped me remember things and enjoy the class more than usual.

It appears that many of the students surveys perceived that teachers did not [r]espect every student no matter the level of knowledge that the student may have." Another trait that students reported was teachers often confuse students,

"She explains to the class in a way that we can understand and doesn't show off with dictionary talk- they don't have to pretend just because they are teachers." The students want to be asked questions so the teacher knows or not if the students understand the material. Although not all teachers want student participation, students want teachers to "[a]ddresses the class while teaching and ask for feedback. Wants the students to pitch in and feel comfortable doing it. It's so much easier to learn that way." Also, "feel the environment OK for you to ask questions."

Hughes, Romeo, and Romeo argue, "When the classroom feels comfortable enough for each person to relax, then students from various backgrounds can take the risk of expressing their views, resulting in a richer blend of perspectives" (411). One way to address diverse cultures in a classroom is to let students see their images in the curriculum by selecting readings that reflect student population (Banks 466). Classroom attrition often results from "wide [cultural] discrepancies in the academic achievement of groups as Blacks and mainstream White youths, between Mexican American and Japanese American students" (452).

Question: 14 asked "What does a poor teacher do while teaching?"

The statements below are a selected representation of all the responses on the surveys.

Get mad with the students when they do not understand the lecture.

A poor teacher degrades the students by making them feel incompetent.

Doesn't care about the students opinion.

A poor teacher doesn't really know how to give the information to the student in a way that they understand it.

Cares only about getting the grades in and pleasing the administration instead of teaching.

Talks about students qualities.

Often teachers do not understand who their students are, where they come from, or their culture (Ybarra 168). Students know when the teacher understands her students, hears and listens to what they tell her, and when she does not. "When teachers fail to recognize the cultural differences among learning styles, students react in negative ways to the instruction" (Ortiz and Garcia qtd. in Oxford and Anderson 201). Students become frustrated, angry, suspicious, and mistrust school systems when teachers do not understand minority cultures. This mistrust is not unusual with Hispanic and other minority students. Many students believe that something is wrong with them when they cannot please instructors, so they feel their only option is to drop the class, or to drop out of school, although not all students do. The result is a high rate of attrition because most professors do not attempt, or know how to try, to intervene to prevent drop out (Canabal 157-167). Mexican Americans are often silenced by instructors overlooking them both in the classroom (Losey 1).

Question: 15 asked "What does a good student do when learning new material?"

The quoted statements below are a selected representation of all the responses on the surveys.

Study right after the teacher has taught new materials to get a better understanding.

The student should takes notes read the chapters from which the lecture was about and let the professor see their work before deadline and attend the study session.

He try to learn and explore himself seek the answers he is having in his mind and maintain regularity.

Re-use the material learned, ask questions when unable to do the new material.

They listen the teacher, try to understand materials, only interrupt class only if it is important and try the best to do work right.

Ask questions if not during class stay after class and talk to your professor.

Many academics fail to associate a student's performance levels with their cultural background, and cultural learning styles. Minority students who graduate from high school and enter college or university are often underprepared to successfully perform in first semester courses (Kolodny par. 1-6). What students learn at home is culture driven and plays an important part in determining how students have learned to learn. When that style is not the same as the school learning style, the student is expected to change to agree that of the school (Swisher and Deyhle 345). One of the things the student needs to learn is how home discourse is similar to and different from Standard American English and academic English and how to shift between the two whenever she wants or needs to. Also, "[t]hey need to learn, for example, to be critical readers and writers, to state claims they can support persuasively, to deal with conflicting points of view in texts, and to re-present those ideas in texts to achieve their own purposes" (Hagemann 75).

Question: 16 asks "What does a poor student do when learning new material?"

The quoted statements below are a selected representation of all the responses on the surveys.

He doesn't maintain regularity and does not even have any question.

Doesn't listen doesn't ask questions, and is to involved with something else.

Does not pay attention, talks and disrumpes other students trying to learn.

Thinks he/she will remember just by hearing once.

Get's angry because they simply can't understand the material, doesn't ask for help to anyone.

Talks during lecture always interrupts class to tell joke or a stupid question, and makes up excuses to not do the work.

He won't bother to say anything because either he's embarrassed or he just doesn't care.

Apparently these students feel like misfits and do not know how to articulate their problem. These are

> language minority students who typically speak various Englishes that are considered nonstandard, the transition [from home to college] is much more difficult. The rules of their home discourses don't overlap as much [as those from middle class English literate homes] with those of the academic world. As a result, many language minority students struggle with the rules and conventions of speaking and writing "school talk." (Hagemann 75)

There are many embedded cultures in the United States that do not stem from foreign countries. These American cultures all have their own language, as Latino English, Puerto Rican English, Vietnamese English or Black English. Some tongues are rural and regional as Appalachian English and urban poor working class. As with any dialect, each has its own grammar system, accent, and intonation and rhythms. Students from these backgrounds come to college with big hopes, but they know they do not speak Standard English which colleges require. Nevertheless, many students have "a native's intuitive sense of what's grammatical in his home language" (Hagemann 75). Therefore, they read English poorly, and their "essays sound very oral, and he pays little attention to punctuation" or grammar (75). These students tend to emphasize the oral side of learning as lectures and study groups. McAndrew and Hurlbert suggest that teachers allow students to spell according to their phonetic sensibilities while focusing on more important errors. This would take the pressure off students to perform while learning to correct their more serious errors (5-7).

Question: 17 asks "What does an English teacher do to make the class a good class?"

The quoted statements below are a selected representation of the surveys. He or she should show the beauty of the language and discusses different topics, gives explanations.

Work with individuals and have one-on-one talks.

Explain us all the material like if we never heard it before.

She/he teaches their class with interesting things not just writing storys w/out explaining them.

Makes real life examples make the student understand the good and bad skills about writers its determining to make the students learn and understood.

Have passience with the students that lack of grammar.

Many high school graduates enter college or university underprepared to successfully perform in first semester courses. Cultural awareness and learning styles may make teachers realize that not every one learns as the teacher does which may inspired her to use various teaching styles (Mangan par. 1-8). Instructors may want to embrace the diversity of a multicultural classroom. One way to show respect is to correctly pronounce names and not change Jorge to George or Martinez' to Martin'ez (Perez 151). Also, teachers may show respect by not to trying to force them to give up their language which, in many cases, be their only connection to their culture. Also, "cognitive and academic skills transfer across languages[. . .] . A curriculum that uses content from a variety of cultures presents a more accurate version of the whole of human experience" (Perez 152).

Question: 18 What does an English teacher do to make an English class a boring class?

The quoted statements below are a selected representation of all the surveys.

Blah! blah! blah! and doesn't stop to explain.

Make the class static not offer student freedom to gain from the class by making grades set on teachers personal philosophy.

100% lecture and assignments using complicating words.

Lecturing without accepting any comments from the students.

Talk through the whole class period and then at the last 5 minutes of the class give an assignment.

Book work and readings anyone can do busy work, no new info. is learned from a text that's way we have teachers.

The emotional climate of the classroom is very important, and the teacher will want to be very sensitive and look for students who appear apprehensive or anxious. A quiet student may be inadvertently made to feel excluded or ignored, or as Losey calls it "silenced" (2). In a predominately Anglo/European classroom, Mexican Americans are often silenced by instructors overlooking them (1). "In comparison to the women, the men were silenced in interaction around course assignments" (Losey 134). Losey noticed that Mexican American men seemed to be intimidated with writing and were effectively silenced. However, Mexican Americans overall wrote more revisions than the Anglo American subjects, and Mexican American women wrote more of them (145). Although writing silenced Mexican American men, classroom discussion silenced Mexican American women. Women did speak some, but not as often nor as loudly as the men. Women seemed to remain silent in deference to the men (156). In Losey's study, the interplay of several factors, including ethnicity, gender, and linguistic barriers silenced Mexican American students. Student answers revealed this practice might be taking place in some classrooms.

Question: 19 Do you think Hispanic teachers make good role models? Why or why not?

The quoted statements below are a selected representation of all the responses on the surveys.

Yes, because we the spanics, see that it she made it threw college so can we.

Definately yes, if a "Hispanic" can teach a college level course, what are my "boundaries".

Yes, because when I was in elementary I only had anglo teachers, and if I was going to go into teaching I would won't to be a hispanic teacher.

Yes, Hispanics tend to be stereotyped as not having a hispanic teacher already proves this stereotype wrong.

Yes, you can't blame your ethnicity for failure.

Since a large number of students surveyed stated that they feel more comfortable with a teacher of the same ethnicity, maybe this means that there should be a greater effort on the part of the English Department to hire more Hispanics teachers. It should be noted that the majority of the responders answered that ethnicity did not matter to them, but good teaching does. This means that Losey's "cultural mismatch theory" (11) is wrong for this University. The theory states that when the culture of the teacher does not match to dominate culture of the class, the students may not be able to fulfill the expectations of the teacher and they "misread" the behavior of the teacher.

Question: 20 What does your family think about your attending college?

The quoted statements below are a selected representation of all the responses on the surveys.

Since I am the first in the whole family to attend college, they are very proud of me.

I am first to graduate high school to. I don't work fields any nore.

Excited, I'm the only one in college or in a high education level.

They are very proud of me, because my mother nor father attend college.

Some laughed at me others are proud I decided to come to college.

My mother is very proud of my since I am the first generation to attend it's what they have always wanted. No one can take your education from you.

Most of the students in English 1301 First-Year Composition fall in the Dualistic category which means that a family has been in the US for a period of time; the adults speak Spanish, but the children speak both English and Spanish. The immediate family remains very important. In addition to the extended family, peer groups grow in influence, and adults in the community become less of a role model. Over time a family becomes Assimilated. This means the primary language is English, the immediate family is still a dynamic force in their lives, but the clan effect dissipates and no longer has a strong influence on relationships. Over time, students become more competitive and achievement oriented as their Anglo-American counterparts (Jimenez 16).

Students enrolled in First-Year Composition feel they need support and acceptance both from their parents and their teachers. Most students are excited to be in college because they are the first generation in their family to achieve this. Moreover, they see the opportunities that a college education will give them. However, in English class, they feel insecure and intimidated because, for many, English is their second language. Students want teachers to be interested in them as a class and as individuals, and to understand their backgrounds. They believe that more one-on-one sessions can help them to learn difficult concepts and to have their questions answered. Often they are too shy or insecure to ask questions in class, but they feel more secure in the privacy of a one-on-one session with their teacher.

While most students state that a role model can be a successful person from any ethnicity and background, many students believe they can feel more relaxed and can learn more from a teacher who has the same culture as their students. Although it is a fallacy, most Hispanic students believe that success in anything is a "natural" for a Caucasian, but not for a Hispanic. Therefore, when Hispanic students see Hispanic teachers, they feel inspired to succeed as those teachers have. Consequently, many Hispanic students seek out Hispanic teachers, not only as English teachers, but in other subjects, as well.

Faculty Surveys

Of the 21 teachers who taught First-Year Composition Spring Semester 2001, eight allowed me to survey their students and six completed instructor surveys. Not all teachers responded to all questions.

Question One: Describe how you teach writing in your classes.

Review mechanics. Eight in-class essays. Preparation outside and in classroom workshops. Limited outline allowed. All essays personal experience–new topic/subject each time. Strict thesis, topic sentence format required.

(1) explain writing process: plan, write, revise; (2) discuss writing strategies, (3) read and discuss samples of professional and student writings; (4) provide writing prompts for students to practice; (5) provide evaluation and feedback of student writings.

Workshop approach, emphasis on high-interest writing topics, fairly lenient grading of essays, and prep for dept. final exam.

I ostensibly follow modes (because that is the way textbook is organized), but I emphasize consistent support of a thesis in whatever form that may take.

I teach writing as a process, using peer evaluation and grouping activities for editing.

First they do freewriting, then they write their first draft. When they have completed the first draft, then they read what they wrote, and to begin to edit. After that they write a second draft that is graded. They use this process for all ten essays they write during the semester.

    I wanted to know how the teachers met the learning style needs of the students. While a general theory will always have individual exceptions, most recent Hispanic immigrants, as is much of the student body of the University, are Field Dependent learners. As the immigrants become assimilated into the American culture, they develop into Field Independent learners, which most Anglo-Americans are and teachers tend to prefer (Jimenez 17).

    There are myriad of cultural differences in a classroom of Hispanic students. This can aid the teacher in selecting teaching styles. Hispanic students are often underprepared for college because of sociodemographic variables of lower economic status and requisite hours of employment often (Canabal 157-167).

    Question Two: How would you describe the students in your class?

(1) some prepared, some not; (2) some interested, some not; (3) some motivated; some not; (4) most are shy about their own writing; (5) most are weak in grammatical training; (6) most lack experience.

The usual mix: the ones we enjoy, the ones whom we can't help and who don't want our help, and everything in between.

Fairly average or below average students from a non-English as first language culture (Mexican-American in Texas).

Uninformed about rules of grammar and basic organizational techniques; heavy background in creative writing; unfamiliarity with English sentence structure and vocabulary.

Students are generally bilingual with Spanish as their mother tongue. Also, they are generally not your typical freshmen; that is, they are usually "older" students.

I wanted to see if teachers made allowances for the possible various cultures in their classrooms. Students are generally capable even if they have language use problems. Garza asserts lack of preparedness would take into consideration the elements which differentiate the many individuals of the same cultural group such as Hispanics who identify themselves as Mexican Americans versus Chicanos, different races who speak the same language because culture is not always affiliated with race, country of origin Mexico versus El Salvador, generation in the United States as fifth generation Mexican Americans versus recent immigrants, level of assimilation, socio-economic status as middle class versus poor inner city. Socio-economic status is one of the most important variables, because it determines much in the way of lifestyle, education, and power. Also, language proficiency as bilingual Hispanic versus monolingual (English or Spanish). (Garza 25-26)

Question Three: What problems do your students face?

The confusion of switching between two languages.

Overcoming ESL-type problems, not knowing exactly what kinds of questions to ask in class and usual grammar, vocab, etc.

Lack of background in English grammar and usage; English as a second language. (1) insufficient training in the grammar of language; (2) lack of confidence.

The greatest problem is the "fear" of writing because they have never been free to write and learn from mistakes. Revision is not a concept they are familiar w/. Language is sometimes a problem with those who are open to revision and helping one another learn.

Getting over the fear of thinking totally in English so as not to make as many grammar mistakes.

I asked this question to learn if the teachers were sensitive to their student's needs. If teachers do not understand minority cultures, students may become disenfranchised, blame themselves for not meeting the teacher's expectations, and feel their only option is to drop the class, or to drop out of school. This attitude is not unusual with Hispanic and other minority students. Teachers should try to understand who their students are, where they come from, or their culture (Banks168).

Question Four: What kind of student has been your best student?

Good oriented, articulate, imaginative–usually those who <u>least need</u> this class.

Can't really say, since I'm thinking mostly of beginner type comp. classes.

The student who has matured, who will work hard, and who is motivated usually makes the best student.

A student who has the typical problems (cited above), but one who has an absolute determination to do well combined with good thinking skills.

The one who is willing to take risks in writing.

Classroom retention results from the teacher motivating and stimulating students and bringing out their strengths. In order to do this, the instructor must recognize these strengths. Classroom attrition often results from instructors not acknowledging cultural differences. There are "wide discrepancies in the academic achievement of groups as Blacks and mainstream White youths, between Mexican American and Japanese American students" (Ybarra 452). To retain students Ybarra suggests that teachers recognize the variety of learning, cognitive, and motivational styles that students bring to the classroom. Also, all students bring certain traits associated with specific ethnic and social-class groups. This challenges the teacher to use a variety of teaching styles to appeal to diverse students. (Ybarra 466)

Question Five: What kind of student has been your worst student?

His complete communication dynamic is grounded in another language–little or no motivation to make the transition.

Immature students who do not attend class, do not buy the text, are not motivated, are the difficult ones.

Those who only attend my classes irregularly, and then expect to make a C on the final exam.

One who is totally unmotivated and has a complete disdain for learning, work, and the classroom.

The one who comes straight from high school and thinks he/she is "hot stuff."

I wanted to learn if teachers believed the student they described as their worst type behaved the way they did because of a cultural learning style clash with the instructor, or from lack of immaturity, or another reason. Culture is a big influence on learning style. Oxford and Anderson found eight different learning styles, most of which can be traced to cultural behavioral preferences when they studied African-American, Greek-American, Chinese-American, Mexican-American, Hawaiian-American, Navajo-American, and Anglo-Saxon-American students. Teachers can adjust their teaching style to reach students of various cultures when they understand the cultural differences (201-215). For instance, Native American students cannot react assertively, respond verbally in class, or make direct eye contact because their culture considers these behaviors impolite (Henderson 47-55). Schools with Native American students should provide quiet times for thinking, and emphasize visual stimuli imagery because they value and develop clear-sightedness, use imagery, perceive globally (Guild 17). Not addressing the student's learning style may result in the student dropping courses or withdrawing from school.

Question Six: Do you use Hispanic authors in your course? If you use Hispanic authors, which authors do you use?

Yes, Richard Rodriguez.

No.

Yes, I use the ones that are featured in the essay samples in the composition texts that I happen to select on a given semester. For example, Richard Rodriguez and Judith Ortiz and Ernesto Galanza are in the present text.

Yes, those in the composition text, such as Richard Rodriguez and Sandra Cisneros.

Yes, I use student papers as my primary source.

Yes, if they are part of the readings in the text.

I asked this question to ascertain if teachers were bringing diversity into their curriculum in an effort to stop student attrition. A curriculum that uses content from a variety of cultures presents a more accurate version of the whole of human experience" (Perez 152). When students can see their culture reflected in the curriculum, they feel included (Ybarra 466). One way to address diverse cultures in a classroom is to select readings that reflect student population.

Question Seven: Describe what you think good teaching is.

Proving to the student that he/she can write well in English.

Prove to the student there is a valid purpose for the course and continue to show that everything that happens in the class serves that purpose.

Student-centered teaching works well for composition classes. The student needs to become part of the writing process in a non-threatening environment. The student needs to feel a sense of growth and accomplishment and that the goals and expectations are possible.

Being well-prepared and on time for each and every class meeting. Try to be fair with every one in class and refrain from boring personal stories.

Good teaching enables the student to understand the relevance of the material/learning to his own well-being.

Allowing student to learn through the process of revision and editing along w/ fellow classmates and instructor.

I wanted to know if these teachers could relate to their students as Mr. D, the teacher in Victor Villanueva's book. He states, "Mr. D could speak *with* us. To speak of Julius Caesar was to speak of how fighting, ganging up, was seen as a solution for many people over a long time. But the power really depended on knowing how to use language, the language of Mark Antony, for instance. Mr. D provided the spark that would flare again some thirteen years later" (3). Teachers strive to inspire students, but they seldom know how well they succeed as many times it takes many years to manifest.

Because literature teachers often do not receive training to teach writing, they do not know how to help a student who can speak well, but cannot write well. Language has two major functions: speaking and writing. Not all oral strategies can be transferred to the writing process, but some aspects of oral language, as expression, is in written language. One reason for poor writing is ethnic word use and non-standard pronunciation. One way to improve teaching of writing is to show the relationship of oral language to writing. Another strategy is to allow students to emphasize their cultural differences. Foreign students need to training the ear to hear correct grammar, then transfer that to writing. Teachers need to take full advantage of the tutors at the Writing Center with instructions for students to learn to recognize the correlation between oral and written language (Sterling 15-20).

Question Eight: What are the goals for your Composition class?

Learn what it takes to communicate for real world compelling purposes at the time (not later) those purposes present themselves.

I hope the student can learn something about organization, structure, correct grammar, development of an idea, support for an idea and overall effective delivery so that the student can write effectively and with confidence.

(1) For students to pass the Dept. Final Exam, (2) To have everyone working 2 to 3 times faster in May than they did in Jan.

Goals: Provide comfortable, "safe" (non-threatening) environment

    Foster confidence about writing

    Provide constant opportunity for thinking/writing

Enable student to internalize the writing process/concept of thesis and organization

To become a fluent writer.

    The purpose of this question is to learn if Losey's "cultural mismatch theory" (11) applies. She argues that most Anglo/European American teachers favor the mainstream, middle-class student by using the Initiation-Response-Evaluation (IRE) technique. Middle-class students often have an advantage because their families use the IRE teaching style with children at home. The poorer student will detect a mismatch in the classroom climate and senses that her background is at fault. It becomes clear that she is at a distinct disadvantage. The end result, is the situation silences her and she refuses to speak out or join in classroom discussion. This is especially true when they do not speak Standard English, as "working class Anglo and rural black families, Native Americans, ethnic Hawaiians, inner city black youths, and [. . .] bilingual Chicanos" (10). For these students, teachers will want make the classroom less threatening and a more level playing field for all ethnicities.

    Question Nine: Why do you want your students to learn to write correct English?

It opens doors for them, gives them confidence; the alternative is unacceptable (applies to any language's culture).

The student needs this basic ability so that he can have success in other academic work and ultimately in the professional world.

It's expected of them on almost every job outside the Valley, as well as on many here in LRGV.

It is the only way that they can become confident members of the academic community.

(1) To communicate in the "real" world; (2) As a step toward their degree.

If they want to be successful in business, they need to be literate in English.

To help prepare students for the "real world" the faculty will want to expose their students to formal, written, standard American English. Also, they need examples of professional type writing to motivate students to become confident in writing English competently for their profession. These students need

> "to be critical readers and writers, to state claims they can support persuasively, to deal with conflicting points of view in texts, and to represent those ideas in texts to achieve their own purposes. [. . .] They need a detailed awareness of how home discourse is similar to and different from Standard American English and an ability to shift smoothly from their home discourse to academic English whenever they want or need to. (Hagemann 75)

Question Ten: What are your hopes and aspirations for your students?

Recognize importance of good communication and the absolute pleasure of it.

I hope the student leaves my composition class as a confident writer who has the ability to succeed in any writing situation and who is competitive with any other writers.

Graduates from UTPA, get a good job, and makes good money.

Become so knowledgeable about the use of language that they have complete confidence in their writing skills.

That they become self-sufficient and leaders.

They become successful in life.

The purpose of this question asks if the goals of the teachers increase student self-confidence and self-esteem. There is a relationship between thinking styles and self-esteem (Zhang and Sternberg 220). This means that students with high self-esteem should also be more self-confident about whatever they do. This self-confidence inspires them to be self-instructed and self-directed. Students with higher self-esteem also tend to prioritize their tasks (220). Teachers could use the relationship of thinking styles with self-esteem by helping them to think creatively when doing assignments. Teachers could use various teaching methods allowing for a variety of thinking and learning styles (220-21).

Question Eleven: What do you like best about living in the Rio Grande Valley?

N/A

The international aspect of the Valley provides an interesting social environment for living.

Having a job at a minority type univ. like UTPA; it's a professional challenge to earn their respect.

Slower pace; diversity.

(1) Living close to Mexico, (2) helping Mexican-American children learn to read and write (high school level)

If the teacher is not happy living here, then they will not be as effective as she could possibly be.

The unique culture of the Valley.

As Miller stated, our Valley is a culture all its own, and as one teacher said, the culture of the Valley is unique. It is like living in a separate country because it is not entirely Mexican or American. "Our southern frontier is not simply American on one side and Mexican on the other. It is a third country with its own identity. This third country [. . .] [is] a colony unto itself [. . .]. (T. Miller xii)

Question Twelve: What do you like least about living in the Rio Grande Valley?

N/A

The heat–the sameness of the weather.

(1) The humidity; (2) The great distances from research libraries; (3) Traffic congestion and air pollution are also a problem for me.

Heat/hot weather; trashy environments (roads, parking lots, neighborhoods).

The poverty and apathy.

The feeling of hopelessness of some of the people.

This question was to elicit the amount of dissatisfaction of the teacher for living on the Mexico-US border. Because this part of the country is so unique, people tend to either love or hate it. For this area, there seems to be no in-between. People often quickly become dissatisfied and leave. As Tom Miller said, "It's a colony unto itself [. . .]" (xii)

Question Thirteen: Do you incorporate the student's oral family history in your classes? If you do, why do you do this, if you do not, why don't you do this?

No, hadn't thought of it, but it might be a very productive writing and research topic.

??? They are only allowed to write about personal experience–family history is often involved. They are encouraged to share the planning of their essays in class discussion–so it can (and does) happen this way.

Yes, the students always have an opportunity to draw from their life bank (oral family history) in their expository writing. Their personal stories always make good writing topics.

YES. (1) It gives the student "ownership" of material to use in writing, and (2) It gives the student a knowledge base from which to begin writing.

No.

Yes and no. Yes if it advances the purpose and topic of the essay, and no when this becomes all the student wants to write about.

I wanted to learn how much of the student's culture was included in the class curriculum. Speaking and writing are the major functions of language which creates a strange relationship between them. Some strategies of oral language, as expression, exists in written language, but not all oral strategies can be transferred to the writing process. Many times the non-standard pronunciation and word use of an ethnic group can interfere with standard writing production. One strategy for improving the teaching of writing is to use the oral-literacy approach by taking advantage of cultures with an oral literacy and show the relationship to writing (Sterling 15-20).

Question Fourteen: What problems do you encounter in teaching Composition?
See #3.

The evaluation of so many essays each semester sometimes becomes difficult because it takes several hours to evaluate each section.

Keeping up with essay-grading load; trying to convince 1301 students that English can be more fun than they think.

Lack of thinking skills/logical organization skills and lack of vocabulary.

The same problems I encountered at The Ohio State University. Students have so much going on [that] 1301 is not always a priority.

Making the students see the value of writing in English, keeping up with the paper workload.

I wanted to learn if the faculty were aware of a mismatch between their teaching style and the learning style of the student.

Sternberg and Zhang describe thinking styles as "a preferred way of thinking or of doing things. A style is not an ability, but rather a preference in the use of the abilities one has" (198), and give evidence that thinking styles may vary from culture to culture. The researchers studied high school and university students in Hong Kong, mainland China, and the United States. They found the reason some students do not perform well in school may be a mismatch between students' thinking styles and the learning style preferred by the teacher. Teachers need to be aware of the thinking style preferred by the predominate culture of the students, and be well educated about thinking styles of both gender and cross-cultural differences (Zhang and Sternberg 211).

Question Fifteen: Do you like to teach Composition? Yes/No Explain the reason for your answer.

Yes/no. I enjoy the successes–I hate the failures.

Yes, I love to teach composition. I love the blending of the creative part of writing with the fixed aspects of it. I love to see the way words and sentences express feelings from the heart and ideas from the mind. I love leading the student into this discovery of self that develops from composition class.

Yes, I love to invent new writing topics and test them out with my 1301 classes. I also like to teach and read the research papers my students write in 1302, where I can learn a good deal about Valley history and culture.

YES, my evaluations are routinely unanimous about my enthusiasm for the subject. I always write with my students, and I attempt to convey in every way possible the power that can be theirs through the written word.

Yes, I feel I have good passing results and have learned a lot w/ available training from La Joya ISD [a town in the western part of Hidalgo County] to help students master passing their 1301 final. I take great joy and pride when my students go on to the next step at the university level. Only 1% of Hispanic women have a college degree; we need more!

YES! Seeing students' faces when they figure out how to do something difficult for them.

If a teacher likes what she is doing, then she will be a more effective teacher. She might become as effective as the teacher Victor Villanueva's Mr. D who "could speak *with* us. [. . .] But the power really depended on knowing how to use language" (3). Villanueva says that Mr. D understands where his students came from; he understands their culture (3). This is what an effective English teacher should be.

Student Interviews
Interview Procedures

Most of the student interviews were conducted in a private classroom in the University Library. Some of the interviews were performed in my private faculty office. Once again, the students were asked to sign a separate Informed Consent Form for the personal interview. I reminded the students that the interview would be audio taped, all answers would be used in a group with no individual identification.

I explained that the questions focused on aspects of teaching that assist learning academic writing, and I wanted to learn which teaching methods do not help their learning, how teachers interact both with the students, and with the course content.

Student Interviews

Of the 282 students surveyed, 53 gave me permission to interview them. I was only able to interview 37 students because either I was not able to reach the student to make an appointment or the student did not keep the appointment when made. I will give the replies of the students interviewed to the questions in groups.

1   In all the English classes that you have taken, what did your favorite teacher do that you liked best?

A large percentage (58%) of the students said the teacher used methods to augment the lecture to show the students how different elements of the lecture fit together. Some drew diagrams on the board, some passed out handouts with the diagrams, a few showed videos, one used "a projector to throw examples from paper to the wall," and one actually drew pictures. Another 18% said they like it when teachers put them into groups to discuss their papers and give peer feedback. While some expressed reluctance to mark other students' work, they felt that discussing the paper made them feel more comfortable. Nine percent liked when teachers told them the relevance of what they were doing in class with a "real life" job, 4% liked in-class essays and the remaining 11% liked a myriad of practices as peer correcting of work, no grammar taught separately from essay writing, no tests, related culturally by including local current jargon and neighborhood events in lectures, one-on-one conferences to discuss each essay with their teacher, and one even included movies from time-to-time.

It appears that the students have the Field Dependent or Field Sensitive Learning Style as described by Jimenez (17). At least 58% of the responders preferred seeing the totality of the concept before focusing in on the specific as a Field Dependent Learner prefers. With a classroom of almost totally Hispanic students, there are myriad of cultural differences within that group that can aid the teacher in selecting teaching styles.

2   In all the English classes that you have taken, what did your favorite teacher do that you liked worst?

The first reply of 62% of the students was teaching grammar. When I asked them to explain, most said that they understood the grammar when taught and usually could pass a test, but the problem came when using it in their own writing. Once the teacher explained the errors using the student's own writing, she seldom made that mistake again.

Another 18% said they did not like it when the teacher called on students to give answers to questions because they did not like speaking out in class. Moreover 4% did not feel comfortable passing their homework or test papers to a peer for grading. Many felt embarrassed, especially when they knew they had not done well. The remaining 16% had no comment.

A large majority (62%) said they did not like the specific teaching of grammar which is task related which is preferred by those who have Field Independent learning style as do most Anglo Americans.

Shuman who was the Director of the Freshman Writing Program at the University of Illinois said,

> I discouraged those who taught in the program from teaching grammar lessons to whole classes. Rather, I encouraged them to discover means of

getting each student to work on his or her problems in usage and mechanics individually. I had found quite early that if I taught a lesson on a topic like subject-verb agreement or the use of the objective case, students who had not had a previous problem in that area would begin to make mistakes in it. Apparently, when they were writing an essay and had a rhetorical decision to make, they frequently half-remembered something that had been said in class a week or so earlier and, unsure of their own abilities, opted for the wrong choice. (15-16)

3   What teaching technique that the English teacher did that helped you the most?

A large portion (42%) stated getting into groups and seeing how other students did the assignment really helped. Another 38% said they liked one-on-one conferences with their teachers, while 14% preferred when teachers allowed multiple draft essays that received feedback from other students. The remaining 6% gave various answers. This again refers to the Field Dependent learning style which most of our Hispanic student body possesses.

4   What teaching technique that the English teacher did that helped you the least?

A majority of 51% said lecturing to the class without allowing questions helped the least. Moreover 28% stated reading the text to the class did not help. Also 11% felt intimidated by writing inclass essays. Another 8% did not like showing student papers that have a lot of errors on a screen. The remaining 2% had a variety of answers. Once again, if a teacher prefers and uses teaching styles preferred by Field Independent Learners to a class filled with Field Dependent Learners, not much learning will take place.

5   Do you like it when teachers put you in a group of 3 or 4 students and you read and give feedback on each other's essays?

More students (38%) liked being put into groups, but 18% did not like group work, and 44% didn't care one way or another. When I asked the 18% who did not like being in peer groups why they felt as they did, they said that they did not trust the input of the group members. The 44% that didn't care said they, too, did not trust their peers, but they understood that they did not have to take their peer's advice. Therefore, it mattered not to them.

This shows that of the students interviewed, Field Dependent learners (38%) and Field Independent learners (44%) dominate. If the teachers want to create a relaxed learning environment, then the instructor will attempt to match her teaching style with her students' Field Dependent learning style because the Field Independent apparently can adapt and don't care which style is used. "When the classroom feels comfortable enough for each person to relax, then students from various backgrounds can take the risk of expressing their views, resulting in a richer blend of perspectives" (Hughes, Romeo, and Romeo 411).

6   What could the teacher do to encourage more class participation?

Most of the responders (58%) stated the teacher should make the classroom more comfortable. When I asked for specifics, the suggestions most often given was "do not dominate the class." I understood that they meant "make the class more of a camaraderie." In other words, the teacher should be the coach, not the judge and jury. But 41% said the teacher should stop lecturing and ask if anyone has any questions or comments more often or in some manner include the students in the discussion more. Again, I asked for explanation and the answer I got most often was small discussion groups where students could compare notes with others to be sure they understood the new material. A couple of students or 1% had no suggestions.

When teachers encourage students to speak without fear of recrimination, students will feel comfortable to speak their views in class discussion. As Hughes, Romeo, and Romeo stated, "When the classroom feels comfortable enough for each person to relax, then students from various backgrounds can take the risk of expressing their views, resulting in a richer blend of perspectives" (411). Of course all students would like an understanding teacher as Victor Villanueva's teacher Mr. D who seems like the ideal teacher because he understands his students' culture and "Mr. D could speak *with* us" (3).

7   What do teachers do to discourage students?

There were a variety of responses; 28% stated that the teacher's superior (I'm better than you poor Mexicans) attitude can make the students feel inferior, while 23% said that some teachers have "pets" who seemingly can do no wrong even when they disrupt the class. Another 19% said some teachers make students "feel stupid" when they ask questions about an assignment or to repeat the directions. But 16% expressed concern about comments written on papers. The students claimed that most teachers write only negative statements on their papers, and that I am one of the few who write compliments as well as constructive comments (some of the students had been in my developmental classes (which can be a prerequisite to 1301 First-Year Composition) previously). While 9% said use, as one female responder said, "high falootin' words." Some students said that the teachers more often than not did not define the words for them, even when they requested itl. The remaining 5% said they had no opinion.

It appears that some teachers expect students to respond in ways that are not comfortable to them because of their culture or their learning style. To emphasize the influence culture has on learning style, Oxford and Anderson found eight different learning styles in seven ethnic groups, most can be traced to cultural behavioral preferences. If teachers understand these cultural differences, they can adjust their teaching style to reach students of diverse cultures (201-215). Another example is if a teacher expects Native American students to react assertively, as many European cultures do, the Native American student will fail because their cultural learning behavior will not permit it (Henderson 47-55). United States schools gear their curricula to the analytical style which the Anglo/European student prefers, "but black people and lower-income people tend to use a predominately relational style" (Claxton and Murrel qtd. in Purkiss 92).

Black students value oral occurrences, physical activities, and loyalty in relationships (Guild 17). All of these concepts effectively discourage students.

8   When teachers write comments on your essays, what do you like least?

A huge percentage (63%) said as one male student "make my paper 'swim' in ink, especially when all the comments are negative." Another 24% did not like the teacher to use abbreviations students did not understand. One student said her teacher "awked all over her essays" and asked me to explain what "awk" means. I asked if she had asked her teacher for an explanation, and she said that she had, but she really didn't understand her. Then I asked if she told her teacher that she still didn't understand, she said that she hadn't because the teacher used too big words and she simply could not comprehend what she said. Of course, I explained what "awk" means and suggested that now she ask her teacher to explain the marks on her paper. Further, 6% didn't like the teacher to use pencil of any color because it makes the teacher look indecisive. However, 4% stated they didn't like when the teacher marks only part of the errors making them think the rest of the essay is error-free when it is not. One student said her teacher made check marks in the margin and she had to find the errors and correct them and return the paper, but she couldn't find the errors because she didn't understand what to look for. The remaining 3% had no comment.

As Shuman stated in his article "Hey, Teacher, You Bloodied up My Paper!" (14), he didn't find grading papers an effective teaching method.

If venting my spleen in bright red ink was good for me (and I doubt that it was), it certainly was not doing much good for many of my students. They wrote week after week, making the same errors in paper after paper. Sometimes I would find a returned paper crumpled up in the trashcan outside my classroom. Obviously, my strenuous efforts at ferreting out every error were wasted on the disheartened and demoralized students who threw their papers away, clearly not having been helped by my meticulous grading. (14)

9   When teachers write comments on your essays, what do you like most?

A majority of the responders (51%) said when the error is not only marked, but there is an explanation of how to fix it. But 36% expressed they wanted to know not only what was wrong in the essay, but what was right, in other words, "when something sounds good or when the example is good, please tell us so" (Responder 22). A few (4%) preferred references to the handbook when marking errors (the teacher could use a code). Another 1% liked it when the teacher put smiley faces, stamps, and stickers on her paper (this was at another university). The remaining 8% had trouble expressing themselves, so they said nothing.

Once again, Shuman stated,

> I sought to emphasize the positive in my comments, pointing to strengths each student had. I made such comments as 'Your use of sensory detail in lines 6 to 11 is excellent' or 'You have a good ear for what people have said in your quotations in line 7 to 9' or 'You make especially strong transitions in paragraphs two, three, and four. What do you think makes them so successful. I was duty-bound to point out illogical or incoherent writing if it occurred, but I found that when I interspersed such criticism with positive statement, students responded well and that, over time, their writing improved, probably because their attitude toward the course became more positive. (15)

10 Do you like it when teachers write a special note on your essays?

Almost every one (93%) said "yes," especially when something nice is said along with the constructive criticism. The other 7% said they didn't care one way or the other.

Not only students, but everyone likes to hear the positive along with the negative. As Shuman said, I sought to emphasize the positive in my comments, pointing to strengths each student had (15).

Conclusion

While most students had no further comments to add, I noticed that all but three interviewees were Hispanic, so I asked all of them if they had an ethnic preference for an English teacher. Twenty-five had no preference other than that the person know how to speak English properly and know how to teacher the subject. Five preferred Anglo Americans, but for different reasons. Three because they thought they knew the language better and, therefore, would be better teachers. One preferred Anglo Americans because he believed that Hispanics could not pronounce the words correctly, and one because his favorite high school English teacher was Anglo American. The remaining seven preferred Hispanics, not because they would be a better teacher, but because they would be good role models.

Since 25 students of the 37 interviewed had no ethnic preference of an English teacher, could this mean that Losey's cultural mismatch theory actually does not apply? It is possible.

Faculty Interviews

Interview Procedures

All of the teachers were interviewed in their faculty office. Each was asked to sign a separate Informed Consent Form for the personal interview. I reminded each teacher that the interview would be audio taped, the questions would be nonthreatening and I let them see the questions before the interview began.

Faculty Interviews

Of the six teachers that answered the survey, four permitted me to interview them; however, two other teachers who did not complete the survey allowed me to interview them.

1   How do you explain what an essay is to students?

One teacher starts with the history of writing and shows how the essay developed from the seventeenth century and the time of Bacon and Plutarch to today. Another instructor begins with writing an essay that he wrote on the board and explaining it to them that essays are a way of organizing discourse. Still another teacher explains essay writing by showing her current students a prior class' essays. Moreover, another teacher shows and analyze essays in the students' text. A different professor says that most students have had essays in high school and think they know what an essay is.

All of these teachers have been teaching many years, and they have very different teaching methods. Because they are successful and popular, they must be addressing their students' learning styles.

Nevertheless, many students who graduate from high school and enter college or university are underprepared to successfully perform in first semester courses. Many academics fail to associate a student's performance levels with their cultural background, and cultural learning styles (Kolodny par. 1-6). Because the various cultures have different value systems, each culture defines for itself what style of learning within its community. The mainstream White American culture values "independence, analytic thinking, objectivity, and accuracy. These values translate into learning experiences that focus on competition, information, tests and grades, and linear logic. These patterns are prevalent in most American schools" (Guild 17-18). Teachers who have ethnic minorities in their classrooms should take these sociodemographic and sociocultural factors into consideration.

2 How do you explain the process of writing to students?

All of the teachers use freewriting, but only five of the teachers teach the process method. Those who teach process start at beginning with strategies to get a topic, narrow it down to subject, come up with a thesis, an introduction and according to the mode, what they are going to do in the essay. Some professors do the prewriting process with their students and then share it with them.

One instructor who teaches in a computer lab uses reader and writer based writing. When the student is comfortable with writer based prose done with the computer monitor off, then she can turn the piece into reader based writing.

Another teacher emphasizes the product and the grades necessary to pass the course. However, a different professor teaches in a computer lab and stresses that students write the first draft of their essay via freewriting with their monitor off. After they have finished the first draft, students may then turn on the monitor and read and begin modifying the draft. He also stresses that all writing is unfinished and correctable and revisable.

All of the responders state that they start the essay process with a freewriting exercise. Although Peter Elbow has not, to my knowledge, said it in so many words, freewriting is a form of orality. Since the first draft of the essay should be writer based writing to get the first draft on the page, it is fitting that it is produced as an oral based freewriting exercise. "From the standpoint of the teacher, the basic fact about the brain is that it is programmed to speak, not to write. Writing, along with reading, was a trick to be learned at the very end of the evolutionary process" (Havelock 353).

3   What do you look for in student writing?

Most said they first look for content and organization. Depending on the teacher, they then look for transitions, punctuation, mechanics, grammar to varying degrees. Some said they, also, look for description that makes the reader feel and experience the essay. One teacher said he grades holistically and looks for a point that is readable with enough sensory material to convince the reader with an authentic voice.

All of the teachers agree on what to look for in an essay. They first look for content, organization, and then other errors. They hope that their students don't run into the problem that Griffin did with his students. They knew what to do, but they had problems doing it (48-49). "Characteristic problems of student persuasive writing include inadequate content, poor organization, and stylistic inappropriateness" (Knudson 14). To help students with organization, Clifford uses feedback sheets that ask specific questions. His feedback sheets for organization includes "What are the parts of this piece? Are the parts related? Should they be? Is the movement of the essay logical? Is there a conclusion? Does it follow what comes before?" (Qtd. in Hillocks 158).

4   What do you consider good writing?

All of the teachers said basically the same thing: readable writing that can make me enjoy reading it and experience it from first sentence with good organization. One instructor said an authentic voice with a point that is readable using a reader response mode. Another teacher added that she looked for something memorable.

Essentially, all composition teachers look for the same things in good writing. Griffin categorized the qualities of good writing as:

> Highly successful: These papers are characterized by a novel central idea, clear organization, adequate and gracefully integrated evidence, natural voice, precise diction, and correct grammar, punctuation, and mechanics.
>
> Moderately successful: Although these papers don't display particularly original thought, their central idea is clearly articulated; their overall organization, though it may break down at times, is clear; their development is adequate though not necessarily graceful, their voice is clear and typically natural, though their diction may be imprecise; and they contain some flaws in grammar, punctuation, and mechanics.
>
> Less-than-successful: These papers typically don't have a clearly articulated central idea; thus their overall organization is unclear; their development is inadequate and/or mechanically presented; their sentences are awkward and their diction imprecise; and they contain serious mistakes in grammar and punctuation. (48-49)

5   How do you deal with students who have difficulty in grasping academic writing?

Everyone said they would have a one-on-one conference with the student. All of these professors use writing texts that present a detailed explanation of the various modes of writing with examples both by students and by professional writers. If after a lecture in class explaining the essay and a teacher/student conference the student still doesn't understand what is expected of her, the most of the teachers would refer the student to the writing center.

The teachers are following the generally accepted premise that
> a familiarity with good or great writing will enhance a writer's own work. A more concrete pedagogical version of this assumption is that a developing writer learns from seeing what others have done and from imitating those forms and techniques. That is, in order to write an essay of a given type, the writer must first be familiar with examples of the type and know the parts of the type and their relationships. [. . .] A few studies did find some statistically significant gains resulting from the use of models. (Hillocks 154-55)

6   How do you encourage class participation?

There are many ways to encourage class participation. First, one professor has topics relevant to students and focuses on content in lecture and essay comments. Another instructor said she uses discussion groups first to get the students talking among themselves about the topic, then they feel freer to speak out in big class discussion. However, some are too shy to ever participate. A different teacher places students into groups to teach grammar and to work through exercises in the text. Still another professor says he only uses workshops to teach essay writing. Nevertheless, everyone agrees that everything is revisable and re-write-able. However, none of the teachers mentioned student participation by speaking out in class discussion.

Most of the students in the University are Hispanic first or second generation US. Therefore, they are field dependent or field sensitive learners who prefer group work (Jimenez 17). It would be foolhardy for a teacher to expect the students to exhibit mainstream White American culture values of "independence, analytic thinking, objectivity, and accuracy. These values translate into learning experiences that focus on competition, information, tests and grades, and linear logic. These patterns are prevalent in most American schools" (Guild 17-18).

7   Do you group students to read each other's essays and give feedback?

All but one of the professors believe in grouping students to read each other's essays and give feedback and all but one of the instructors have used it. Moreover, weaker students can get ideas from reading better essays, and they'll ask each other for help when they won't ask the teacher. However, these teachers do not use it as a regular practice because students tend to socialize and not work. One professor is not big on group work because he believes that students are too insecure to let peers read their work, however, he demands that someone besides the teacher read all essays before he does.

As Jimenez has indicated, most first or second generation Hispanics are field dependent or field sensitive learners who prefer group work (17). Most of the students in the University are first or second generation Hispanic. Peer response groups were first introduced by Peter Elbow in 1973. When first introduced, they were a little known and little practiced technique. Most teachers believed the practice was little more than "the blind leading the blind" (v). Since then theorists and teachers have come to see the value and use of groups in teaching writing, providing there is proper help and instruction in the most effective method in doing so. Nevertheless, "there is something messy and potentially chaotic about using peer groups. [. . .] [W]e sometimes ask students to work in pairs, sometimes in small groups. We sometimes change groups during the course term: often we stick with stable pairs or groups so that students can safely build up trust in each other" (v-vi).

8   When grading essays, what errors do you mark?

Most teachers focus on paragraph organization and major errors. They try not to mark a lot on bad papers, but some students will come and ask questions anyway. If the paper is good, all errors will be marked. Another teacher always uses red ink because she found that the errors are easier to see than green and purple.

One instructor grades no papers because all papers are gone over in a one-on-one conference with the student by his side. He does this for every essay all semester.

All of these instructors are popular with the students, so they must find their teacher's feedback helpful. I don't know if marking the essays or conferencing would be more effective, but the teacher that does the conferencing says that, for him, this method works best. However, the big question is: what errors should be marked.

Theorists have resoundingly recommended emphasizing matters of content, development, focus and organization, and holding off giving any appreciable attention to local matters until the paper has taken shape. They have urged us, further, to view the student's text in light of the larger contexts that inform the writing, taking into consideration such concerns as the assignment, audience and purpose, voice, the background and experience of the writer, the students' writing processes, genre conventions, and institutional standards. (Straub 34)

9   Do you write end notes on essays? Why or why not?

One instructor writes very short notes, but if they want to know more, I'll have a conference with them. Another will tell only what she likes about the paper. But yet another teacher will write only notes saying this is good, do more of this, or give this more emphasis. But no other kinds of notes. I read papers as a reader, not as a teacher.

Regardless of the method used by the teacher, too much should not be written on the paper. The student should not be overwhelmed with marks, good, bad, or a mixture of the two.

The idea here is simple: avoid overburdening students by focusing on only two or three concerns in a given set of comments. Instead of dealing with ideas, development, focus, sentence structure, and usage–all in the same response, deal only with ideas and development or, say, with ideas, development and focus. As Lunsford puts it: "Say enough for students to know what you mean"–that is make the comments you do make and specific. "But don't say too much"–do not take on too many issues or areas of the student's writing. (qtd. in Straub 40).

10   If you write notes, what do you write in them?

One teacher said that he writes what is good in the end note, but he writes critical notes in the margins of the text by the errors. Another instructor said that he writes only positive notes along with calling attention to one or two major errors. He grades very lenient in Sept., harder in Oct., harder still in Nov., and very hard in Dec. Yet, another teacher said he doesn't write notes except good comments in margins. I counsel with each student in a one-on-one conference. Still another teacher said she writes first positive comments in the notes followed by what the student should focus on in the next essay.

It appears that all of the teachers have focused on the student's image of herself as a writer and do not want to hurt the student's self-image. These instructors seem to understand their students and how to help them improve their writing. "A long history of research on response has debated the usefulness of praise. Recently, though, researchers have become more and more convinced of the value of positive comments" (Straub 46).

A general impression is that teachers are meeting most of the students' needs, and the students who attend class, participate in class, and do homework seem satisfied with their teachers and the course. However, there is still the question regarding why students drop the course or do not pass with a grade of C or better.

Chapter 5. Discussion

The purpose of this study was to research the perception of students currently enrolled in English 1301 First-Year Composition and the perception of faculty currently teaching the course to learn if they intuit an ethnic and cultural imbalance between the largely Anglo American faculty and the almost completely Hispanic student body. Additionally for many years, I have heard complaints from both faculty and students about the many times some students have to retake English 1301 First-Year Composition before they are able to pass the course with a C or better. Moreover, I had heard rumors from people outside of the English department and the University speculating that the cause of the student repetitiveness could stem from this cultural mismatch. For this reason, I decided to study the situation and perceptions of currently enrolled students and current faculty teaching the course by first administering a survey in classes that faculty gave permission, and to faculty teaching those classes. Both groups that were surveyed had follow up interviews with those who gave permission.

Student Discussion

When asked what kind of teacher the students prefer, almost all of the them replied that they prefer a teacher with whom they can disagree and who does not get upset easily, but will talk out the misunderstanding. They also liked the teacher who conducts a relaxed classroom. Research by Hughes, Romeo, and Romeo showed that students learn better with a teacher who does not censor them when students state their point of view. Moreover, teachers who try to have classroom discussion will find students more willing to contribute to the discussion.

Students prefer teachers who let students make mistakes and, instead of the instructors degrading their students, the teachers remain calm in a relaxed atmosphere. Moreover, the teacher took time to get to know the students and relate to their backgrounds. What most faculty do not realize is that the concept of a teacher in Mexico is very different from the role of a teacher in the United states. As Guild pointed out, Mexican-American students often develop friendships with their teachers and prefer that instructors take the role of coach, rather than to dominate over the classroom. However, when some students state that a teacher is rude and doesn't treat her students with respect, it could actually be Losey's "cultural mismatch theory" in action. This theory states that there is a mismatch between the teacher's and class' culture which can cause misunderstandings. Given the dominate ethnicity of both the faculty and student body of the Department, Losey's theory was a good possibility.

When asked to describe good teaching, the most interesting answers came in the interviews, but both the survey replies and the interview responses focused on the lecture and clearly explaining the material. A large percentage of the students said they preferred that the teacher use various methods to show how various parts of the lecture fit together. Some said diagrams drawn on the board helped a lot; some liked it when teachers passed out handouts; a few liked videos; one student said she liked seeing "a projector to throw examples from paper to the wall;" and one student stated that the instructor actually drew pictures on the board. As most Hispanics are Field Dependent learners, the students preferred seeing the totality of the concept before focusing in on the specific. A close second choice of the students was getting into groups and conferencing to help each other understand the lesson and give peer response to essays. Many minorities prefer to work in small groups to figure out the material and to work on class projects. Jimenez indicates this is the preferred learning style of Field Dependent Learners which includes a large number of Hispanics.

Most Hispanics abhor speaking out in class and interrupting the teacher to ask questions. It just is against accepted behavior in the Mexican culture. However, a majority of the students who responded to the question have become Americanized enough to say that it no longer bothers them to speak out in class.

After asking the students who makes a good teacher and what teaching style they prefer, I asked them what teaching methods they believe a good English teacher should do in class. Besides showing a passion for the job, and the beauty of the language, in a positive, relaxed environment, the students favor showing concepts on the board, one-on-one conferences, as well as group work. Once again, this coincides with Jimenez' Field Dependent research of Hispanics.

Because some faculty complain that students just sit in class and don't seem to participate at all, I asked the students what the teacher could do to solve this problem.

Most said the teacher should make the classroom more relaxed and comfortable. When I asked for suggestions, most replied "do not dominate the class." I understood that they meant the teacher should be the coach, not the judge and jury. But many students said the teacher should stop lecturing often and ask if anyone has any questions or comments or in some manner include the students in the discussion more. Again, I asked for explanation and the answer I got most often was small discussion groups where students could compare notes with others to be sure they understood the new material before speaking out in class. To address the class before feeling fully confident, most students found embarrassing.

Besides speaking in class, I wanted to learn how students would prefer written feedback from their teacher. Most of the students wanted an explanation written, even if it is a code, along with the error marked. They also wanted the teacher to mark not only what is wrong, but what is right, and very right. By that they mean to tell them when they do something exceptionally right. Then I asked them what they liked written on their papers the least. Students dislike having their paper 'swim' in ink of negative comments. A smaller group of students did not like the teacher to use abbreviations they did not understand, and being afraid to ask the teacher for an explanation. When asked if they liked when teachers wrote a special note on their essays, almost every one said they did, especially when something nice is said along with the constructive criticism.

The final question tested Losey's cultural mismatch theory. I asked if they thought Hispanic teachers make good role models, and I was surprised to learn that an overwhelming majority of the students said that the ethnicity of the instructor didn't matter, as long as she was a good teacher. But the remaining students stated that they felt more comfortable with a Hispanic teacher. When I asked this question at the close of the interviews, I pushed the students to explain why they answered as they did. A few who preferred Anglo Americans stated that they know how to pronounce English properly. Some preferred Anglo Americans because students thought Anglos know the language better and, therefore, would be better teachers. The rest preferred Hispanics, not because they would be a better teacher, but because they would be good role models.

Faculty Discussion

First I wanted to know how the faculty approached teaching writing in their classes and if they were meeting their students learning style. Some of the teachers begin by explaining the writing process, freewriting, and then proceeding to the different modes. Others begin by reviewing mechanics. All faculty said they present professional and student essays for the students to study. Some of them use the workshop approach using peer evaluation and grouping activities for editing.

Next I wanted to learn how the faculty relate the course to their students' culture by using Hispanic authors in their courses. Most faculty, but not all, use the Hispanic authors featured in the essay samples in the composition texts. Some of the authors included are Richard Rodriguez, Judith Ortiz, Ernesto Galanza, and

Sandra Cisneros. However, one teacher said she uses student papers as her primary source of readings.

Because the literature suggests incorporating the student's oral family history into classes to incorporate the student's culture in the class, I wanted to know if this faculty does this. Some faculty say flat out no, but one teacher honestly said no because he/she hadn't thought of it, but it might be a very productive writing and research topic. Another faculty said yes and no. Yes if it advances the purpose and topic of the essay, and no when this becomes all the student wants to write about. They are only allowed to write about personal experience–family history is often involved. They are encouraged to share the planning of their essays in class discussion–so it can (and does) happen this way. But other teachers say the students always have an opportunity to draw from their life bank (oral family history) in their expository writing. Their personal stories always make good writing topics, plus it gives the student "ownership" of material to use in writing, and it gives the student a knowledge base from which to begin writing.

No matter what subject an instructor teaches, there will always be problems. I wanted to learn what this faculty saw as their problems in teaching Composition and how they solved them. At the student level lack of thinking skills, logical organization skills, lack of vocabulary, and language use skills. Also, making the students see the value of writing in English, and trying to convince 1301 students that English can be more fun than they think. One instructor who came to the University from outside Texas said that she encountered the same problems at The Ohio State University; the students have so much going on that 1301 is not always a priority for them. Now for the problems at the faculty level, every teacher named keeping up with essay-grading workload. The evaluation of so many essays each semester sometimes becomes difficult because it takes several hours to evaluate each section.

Since I had asked students what they thought good teaching is, I decided to ask faculty to describe what they thought good teaching is. The most basic reply was to prove to the student there is a valid purpose for this course and continue to show that everything that happens in the class serves that purpose, and also proving to the student that she can write well in English. Student-centered teaching works well for composition classes because the student needs to become part of the writing process in a non-threatening environment. Further, the student needs to feel a sense of growth and accomplishment and that the goals and expectations are possible. This can happen by allowing the student to learn through the process of revision and editing along with fellow classmates and instructor.

Each teacher has different goals for their classes, so I wanted to know what goals these faculty had for their Composition classes. Generally the faculty want students to learn what it takes to communicate for real world compelling purposes at the time, and not later, those purposes present themselves. The faculty wants the student to learn something about organization, structure, correct grammar, development of an idea, support for an idea and overall effective delivery so that the student can write effectively and with confidence. These goals would be accomplished by providing a comfortable, "safe" (non-threatening) environment, fostering confidence about writing, and providing constant opportunity for thinking/writing. This should enable the student to internalize the writing process/concept of thesis and organization, and to become a fluent writer.

In order to learn how the faculty see their students, I asked them to describe their students. One teacher said, "The usual mix: the ones we enjoy, the ones whom we can't help and who don't want our help, and everything in between." This generally stated what all of them said, although some were more specific mentioning students' unfamiliarity with English sentence structure, vocabulary, and basic organizational techniques. Nevertheless, the students are generally capable, even if they have language use problems. All of these elements would translate into general lack of preparedness for college work and problems for both faculty and student.

The primary challenge would be overcoming ESL-type problems of confusion of switching between two languages, lack of background in English grammar and usage, and lack of confidence. This lack of confidence can be manifested in several ways. One could be not knowing exactly what kinds of questions to ask in class, another could be getting over the fear of thinking totally in English so as not to make as many grammar mistakes, but the greatest problem is the "fear" of writing because they have never been free to write and learn from mistakes. Revision is not a concept they are familiar with. Language use is sometimes a problem with those who are open to try revision.

And yet, the best student, quoting a respondent, is "a student who has the typical problems cited above, but one who has an absolute determination to do well combined with good thinking skills." Other attributes of a good student that other faculty mentioned are a good attitude, articulate, imaginative, mature, works hard, motivated and willing to take risks in writing.

The most difficult student is the one who comes straight from high school and thinks she is "hot stuff." Further, she is immature, does not attend class, does not buy the text, is unmotivated, has a complete disdain for learning, work, the classroom, and has her complete communication dynamic grounded in another language with little or no motivation to make the transition. And still she expects to make a C on the final exam.

Since I asked faculty about their goals for their classes, I decided to ask why they want their students to reach their goal of learning to write correct English. First, if they want to be successful in business, they need to be literate in English; it's expected of them on almost every job outside the Valley, as well as on many here in LRGV, and it opens doors for them, gives them confidence; the alternative is unacceptable–and this applies to any language's culture. Moreover, the student needs this basic ability so that he can have success in other academic work and ultimately in the professional world. It is the only way that they can become confident members of the academic community.

All teachers have hopes and aspirations for their students, and I wanted to know what these faculty felt for their students. Teachers want students to leave composition class as a confident writer who has the ability to succeed in any writing situation and who is competitive with any other writers. In addition, the student should recognize the importance of good communication and the absolute pleasure of it that she becomes so knowledgeable about the use of language that she has complete confidence in her writing skills, becomes self-sufficient, a leader, and successful in life. Ultimately that she graduates from UTPA, gets a good job, and makes good money.

Notwithstanding, Tom Miller says that the Lower Rio Grande Valley is not simply the southern border with American on one side and Mexican on the other, but it is a third country with its own identity, I wanted to know how the faculty felt living here. Those that answered the question called attention to the unique culture of the Valley. Also, the international aspect of the Valley provides an interesting social environment for living at a slower pace with diversity. Another liked living close to Mexico, and helping Mexican-American children learn to read and write. Moreover, having a job at a minority type university like UTPA is a professional challenge. It can be difficult to earn the respect of these students. These responses show these teachers are happy living here, so they will be effective instructors.

Nonetheless, living in any location has its drawbacks, so I ask the faculty what they like least about living in the Rio Grande Valley. Once again, not everyone answered the question, but those who did named the sameness of the weather as the major drawback. Specifically, the heat and humidity, and trashy environment (roads, parking lots, neighborhoods). The poverty and apathy and the feeling of hopelessness of some of the people. While there is relatively little traffic congestion and air pollution here, it brought dissatisfaction from one teacher living on the Mexico-US border. Although only one instructor noted it, all faculty lament about the great distances to good research libraries.

Finally, I wanted to learn if this faculty really liked what they are teaching. Every one of the teaches loves and enjoys teaching English 1301 First-Year Composition, but they hate the failures. As one teacher said, "I love the blending of the creative part of writing with the fixed aspects of it. I love to see the way words and sentences express feelings from the heart and ideas from the mind. I love leading the student into this discovery of self that develops from composition class." Also they love seeing students' faces when they figure out how to do something difficult for them. Plus, as one teacher said, "Only 1% of Hispanic women have a college degree; we need more!"

Conclusion

Even though popular thought maintains that should a traditional minority ethnicity become a majority of the student population in a university, then those students should experience academic success. Therefore, since Hispanics are the majority of the student population in the University, then why do so many Hispanic students in a "Mexican University" have to repeat English 1301 First-Year Composition? From my analysis of the responses to my surveys and interviews discussed above the students and faculty do not perceive a cultural mismatch as purported by Losey. Considering that there is not a cultural mismatch, the question remains, why do so many students have to repeat the course? Could Witkin's field-intermediate learners, who need a moderation of what the other two groups need have, any relevancy here (Meng and Patty183)?

According to the responses of the students on the survey and during their interviews, they indicated that their Field Dependent needs as described by Jimenez are being met. Further the responses from the faculty indicate that they are addressing their students' Field Dependent needs. Also, faculty make sure students can see their culture reflected in the curriculum through Hispanic authors as indicated by Perez and Banks.

From my analysis of the data, I cannot detect a clash of the Anglo American faculty with the Hispanic student body; in fact, I would not be surprised that many of the student have made friends with their faculty as Guild pointed out is the practice in Mexico.

What do the students and faculty perceive is the reason for the high repetitive rate in this course at this University? Analysis of the data reveals that both faculty and students attribute the attrition rate to lazy students who do not accept responsibility to attend class, to sleep in class, and to not turn in all homework, and thereby either fail or drop the class.

However, I attribute the repetitive rate to those students who have been in this country long enough to no longer be Field Dependent, but they have not evolved enough to be Field Independent. They are somewhere in between, Field-Intermediate. Apparently, when the faculty teaches to the Field Dependent student who are the vast majority of the class, those students who are "in between" or Field-Intermediate cannot handle the mismatch of teaching style as easily as the fully evolved Field Independent student can.

In 1974, when Witkin identified the Field-Intermediate learners, he only stated that the needs of this groups was a "moderation of the two extreme groups" (Meng and Patty 184). In opposition to Witkin, Meng and Patty found "the needs of the field-intermediate subjects were found to be qualitatively different from those of the extreme groups. Although degrees of field-dependence-independence could be plotted on a continuum, instructional needs could not" (184). Because the academic needs of these students are unknown, the "in betweens" become frustrated and rebel by not participating in class, by not turning in homework, by not paying attention, by sleeping in class, or by not attending class. Thus they either drop the class or do not pass with a grade of C or better.

Additionally, analysis of the faculty perceptions appear that they are happy, like what they are doing, and seem to be effective teachers. It took thirteen years for Villanueva's teacher that he calls Mr. D. to inspire him to become a success. It may take that many years for the seeds that these teachers plant now to take hold. But, as Villanueva says, this is what an effective English teacher should be.

My parents used to tell me that at one time there was a basis for every rumor. The rumors described in chapter one may have been true in the past, but they apparently are not true in this day and time.

For Further Study

If this University is having a problem of so many First-Year students having to repeat First-Year Composition, perhaps other schools with a large minority population have the same situation. Until I undertook this study, the department administrators were not sure why such a large percentage of the students had to repeat the course so many times. However, now that they know what the problem is, the next question is finding a way to prevent those students from dropping out of the course.

Nevertheless, not all minorities have the same learning styles and, therefore, will not have the same problems. Some of the research mentioned in the Review of the Literature section of this study focused on the following Eskimo tribes, Native American tribes, Pacific Islanders, African Americans, Hispanics, among others. All of these minorities have schools where they are either in the majority or are a large percentage of the student population. Moreover, most of these schools probably have faculties that have a majority of a different ethnicity than the student body. When this happens, the possibility of Losey's cultural mismatch theory occurs. Perhaps these institutions could conduct a similar study to learn if their school has the same communication mismatch that the University had or if they have a different problem.

Schools that have predominately Caucasian student bodies usually have all, or mostly, Caucasian faculties. Also, schools with a preponderance of African American students have all, or mostly, African American faculties. However, when it comes to schools that have a large student population of other minorities, the faculty is almost always all, or mostly, Caucasian. Since each minority culture has its own traditions and variations within the culture, the instructor must adapt teaching styles to meet the needs of those students. Even so, teachers are not usually trained to meet minority culture learning styles using diverse teaching strategies not of their own ethnicity. With more and more immigrants from other nations in this country, classrooms are becoming more culturally diverse. Teachers need to be prepared to meet the educational needs of this new classroom. If these needs are not met, more students will, as Henderson argued, drop courses only to repeat them, or withdraw from school.

Moreover, more study needs to be done to make sure that teachers are meeting the needs of the students. The traditional teaching style for Caucasian teachers is to maintain total authority in the classroom and deliver a lecture from behind a podium. But this teaching style usually does not meet the needs of non-European-American cultures and other ethnicities. As Paulo Freire pointed out in his book, <u>Pedagogy of the Oppressed</u>, students from these other cultures respond best in this post-modern world to a liberatory education. This is one where the instructor becomes a facilitator and allows students to contribute as much to the classroom discussion as the teacher does. Freire advocates that students learn best when they can participate in the learning process. Are instructors prepared to participate in the post-modern world and learn to adjust their teaching style to allow students to participate in their learning?

The University that is the focus of this study is nontraditional in that, depending upon the semester, the portion of Hispanics to the total population fluctuates from 80-90%. Many Hispanic college students experience much resistance to their attending school from their families since they are not holding down a full-time job and contributing to the family income. Oftentimes when students drop out of First-Year Composition, they also withdraw totally from school to fulfill the needs of their families. However, a good number of these students are not school drop outs, but they are school "stop outs" in that a large portion of them return to school after a period of time. When they return, these older students have different needs than the younger students. These students have the same cultural needs as the younger students, but they also have more life experience. Therefore, this additional life experience often changes their learning style to their school studies. Are teachers trained to meet the cultural and learning style differences of these students?

The University in this study has become a prototype for Hispanic studies. It appears that this study has created more questions than it has answered. The study answered the question of why some students repeat First-Year Composition so many times, and it identified who these students probably are, the "in-betweeners," or Field Intermediates. But this creates many more questions, as is there an alternative discourse to reach the "in-betweeners," or Field Intermediates, to prevent them from becoming discouraged and dropping out of First-Year Composition? Perhaps a survey similar to the one used in this study conducted during the first week of school may help to identify those students who are fall into the category of "in-betweeners." What metamessage are teachers sending students by not addressing their needs by adjusting their teaching methods? Is there a hidden meaning when professors suggest that students drop the course because they are failing, instead of attempting to help the student with one-on-one tutoring, or another teaching strategy? What teaching method will be most productive in meeting the needs of the in-between students learning style? Are there different categories for the different stages of evolution from Field Dependent to Field Independent? Assuming there are categories, what would they be called? How would they be described?

Since the in-between students are evolving to Field Independent learning style, are there alternative measures that would fulfill their learning needs? For example, could they benefit from a computer based composition class taught in a computer laboratory or classroom? Most First-Year students have had computer experience with many different types of computer games at home and in arcades.

Could taking a First-Year Composition class using a computer address the learning style needs of the "in-betweener", or Field Intermediate? One teacher who participated in this study believes that this could well be the answer to this problem.

Further, the in-between student is moving toward being more independent and able to work more independently, rather than in a group. Is it possibly that some of these students could be mature and self-disciplined enough to take the First-Year Composition course as a Distance Learning course and seeing the instructor in a classroom with the rest of the students only once a semester? Of course, all of the students are encouraged to contact the teacher for one-on-one conferences from time to time, but most of the time the distance learning students work independently. Would some of these in-between students be able to handle such a class?

All of these questions and more could be answered with further study.

Bibliography

Amastae, Jon. <u>Language Shift and Maintenance in the Lower Rio Grande Valley of South Texas</u>. Edinburg, Texas: Pan American University, 1978.

Arevalo, Rodolfo. "University Second in Nation in Hispanic Student Enrollment." <u>Los Arcos</u>. 7.3 Spring/Summer 2001: 4.

Banks, James A. "Ethnicity, Class, Cognitive, and Motivational Styles: Research and Teaching Implications." <u>Journal of Negro Education</u>. 57.4 (Fall 1988): 452-466.

Barnhardt, Carol. "Life on the Other Side: Native Student Survival in a University World." <u>Peabody Journal of Education</u>. 69.2 (Win 1994): 115-39.

Bertini, Mario, Luigi Pizzamiglio, and Seymour Wapner, eds. <u>Field Dependence in Psychological Theory, Research, and Application: Two Symposia in Memory of Herman A. Witkin</u>. Hillsdale, NJ: Lawrence Erlbaum Associates, Publishers, 1986.

Canabal, Maria E. "Hispanic and non-Hispanic White Students Attending Institutions of Higher Education in Illinois: Implications for Retention." <u>College Student Journal</u>. 29.2 (June 1, 1995): 157-167.

Cantu, Norma E. "Living on the Border: A Wound That Will Not Heal." <u>Borders and Identity</u>. Ed. Smithsonian. Washington, D.C., 1996.

Carli, Renzo, Franco Lancia, Rosa Maria Paniccia. "Implications of Field Dependence for Social Psychology." Bertini, Pizzamiglio, and Wapner 63-83.

Cho, Mika and Edward Forde. "Designing Teaching and Assessment Methods for Diverse Student Populations." <u>Journal of Art and Design Education</u>. 20.1 (2001): 86-95.

Cisneros, Jose. <u>Borderlands: The Heritage of the Lower Rio Grande through the Art of Jose Cisneros</u>. Edinburg, Texas: Hidalgo County Historical Museum, 1998.

Davidson, Barry S. et al. "How to meet the Needs of the Community College Diverse Adult Student Population." <u>Journal of Adult Education</u>. 18.2 (Spring 1989): 25-31.

Dillon, J. T. "Using Diverse Styles of Teaching." <u>Journal of Curriculum Studies</u>. 30.5 (Sept. 1, 1998): 503-514.

Dreher, Sonja. "Learning Styles: Implications for Learning and Teaching." <u>Rural Educator</u>. 19.2 (Winter 1997): 26-29.

Dunn, Kenneth John, and Edmund R. Frazier. "Teaching Styles." <u>Reading, Writing, and Learning Disabilities</u>. 6.3 (July 1, 1990): 347-367.

Dunn, Rita. "Capitalizing on College Students' Learning Styles: Theory, Practice, and Research." <u>Practical Approaches to Using Learning Styles in Higher Education</u>. Westport, CN: Bergin and Garvey, 2000.

Elbow, Peter, and Pat Belanoff. <u>Sharing and Responding</u>. 3rd ed. New York:McGraw-Hill, 2000.

Erickson, Bette LaSere, and Glenn R. Erickson. "Working with Faculty Teaching Behaviors." Improving Teaching Styles. Ed. Kenneth E. Eble. San Francisco: Jossey-Bass Inc. 1980. 57-67.

Frisby, Craig L. "One Giant Step Backward: Myths of Black Cultural Learning Styles." School Psychology Review. 22.3 (1993): 535-58.

Garza, S. Ana. "Teaching Language Minority Students: An Overview of Competencies for Teachers." Teacher Education Quarterly. 18.2 (Spr. 1991): 23-36.

Goodenough, Donald R. "History of the Field Dependence Construct." Bertini, Pizzamiglio, and Wapner 5-13.

Grant, Heidi, and Carol S. Dweck. "Cross-Cultural Response to Failure: Considering Outcome Attributions with Different Goals." Farideh Salili, Chi Yue Chiu, and Ying Yi Hong, eds. Student Motivation: The Culture and Context of Learning. New York: Kluwer Academic/Plenum Publishers, 2001. 203-19.

Griffin, C. Williams. "Improving Students' Writing Strategies: Knowing Versus Doing." College Teaching. 46.2 (Spring 1998): 48-52.

Griggs, Shirley, and Rita Dunn. "Hispanic-American Students and Learning Style." Emergency Librarian. 23.2 (Nov.-Dec. 1991): 11-16.

Guild, Pat. "The Culture/Learning Style Connection." Educational Leadership. 51.8 (1994): 16-21.

Hagemann, Julie. "A Bridge from Home to School: Helping Working Class Students Acquire School Literacy." English Journal. 90.4 (2001): 74-81.

Havelock, Eric A. "Orality, Literacy, and Stars Wars." Written Communication: An International Quarterly of Research, Theory, and Application. 15.3 (July 1998):351-60.

Henak, Richard M. "Addressing Learning Styles." The Technology Teacher. 52.2 (Nov. 1, 1992): 23-28.

Henderson, James C. "Minority Student Retention." New Directions for Community Colleges. (Summer 1991): 47-55.

Hillocks, George, Jr. Research on Written Communication. Urbana, IL: ERIC Clearing House on Reading and Communication Skills and the National Conference on Research in English, 1986.

Hughes, Diane, and George C. Romeo. "Enhancing Multiculturalism for Nontraditonal Students." College Student Journal. 33.3 (1999): 407-413.

Hutchinson, Lynn M., and Mary E. Beadle. "Professors' Communication Styles: How They Influence Male and Female Seminar Participants." Teaching and Teacher Education. 8.4 (1992): 405-418.

Jimenez, Ricardo. "Understanding the Culture and Learning Styles of Hispanic Students." Momentum. 14.1 (Feb 1983): 15-18.

Johnson, Marjorie. "Historic Rio Grande Valley: An Illustrated History." San Antonio: Historical Publishing Network, 2001.

Khirallah, Michael. "Harklau, L., Losey, K. M., and Siegal, M. (Eds.). (1999).Generation1.5 Meets College Composition: Issues in the Teaching of Writing to U.S.-Education Learners of ESL." Studies in Second Language Acquisition. 22.4 (2000): 599-600.

Killingsworth, M. Jimmie. "Product and Process, Literacy and Orality: An Essay on Composition and Culture." College Composition and Communication. 44.1 (1993): 26-39.

Knudson, Ruth E. "College Students' Writing: An Assessment of Competence." The Journal of Educational Research (Washington, D.C.). 92.1 (Sept./Oct. 1998): 13-19.

Kolodny, Annette. "Colleges Must Recognize Student's Cognitive Styles and Cultural Backgrounds." The Chronicle of Higher Education. Feb. 6, 1991 <http://chronicle.com/che-data/articles.dir/articles-37.dir/issue-21.dir/21a04401.htm>.

Levy, Jack, Theo Wubbels, Mieke Brekelmans, and Barbara Morganfield. "Language and Culture Factors in Students' Perceptions of Teacher Communication Style." International Journal of Intercultural Relations. 21.1 (Feb 1997): 29-56.

Losey, Kay M. Listen to the Silences: Mexican American Interaction in the Composition Classroom and the Community. Norwood, NJ: Ablex Publishing Corp., 1997.

Mangan, Katherine S. "Colleges Offer Faculty Help in Understanding Students." The Chronicle of Higher Education. Mar. 6, 1991 http://chronicle.com/che-data/articles.dir/articles-37.dir/issue-25.dir/ 25a01102.htm>.

McAllen Chamber of Commerce. Facts about the Area. McAllen, Texas: McAllen Chamber of Commerce, 2000.

McAndrew, Donald A., and C. Mark Hurlbert. "Teaching Intentional Errors in Standard English: A Way to "big smart english." English Leadership Quarterly. (1994).

McDonald, Archie P. "The Treaties of Velasco." TexasEscapes.com. <http://www.texasescapes.com/AllThingsHistorical/TreatiesOfVelascoAM803.htm>.

McGlynn, Angela. "Hispanic Women, Academia, and Retention." Hispanic Outlook in Higher Education. 8.12 (Feb. 1, 1998): 12-14.

Meng, Karen, and Del Patty. "Field Dependence and Contextual Organizers." Journal of Educational Research. 84.3 (January/February 1991): 183-189.

Miglietti, Cynthia L., and C. Carney Strange. "Learning Styles, Classroom Environment Preferences, Teaching Styles, and Remedial Course Outcomes for Underprepared Adults at a Two-Year College." Community College Review. 26.1 (Summer 1998): 1-19.

Miller, Hubert J., and Almaraz, Felix D., Jr. "Four Centuries of Shared Experience in the Borderlands." Borderlands: The Heritage of the Lower

Rio Grande through the Art of Jose Cisneros. Jose Cisneros. Edinburg, Texas: Hidalgo County Historical Museum, 1998.

Miller, Tom. On the Border. Tucson: The University of Arizona Press, 1981.

Miville, Marie L., Danel Koonce, Pat Darlington, and Brian Whitlock. "Exploring the Relationships Between Racial/Cultural Identity and Ego Identity among African Americans and Mexican Americans." Journal of Multicultural Counseling and Development. 28.4 (Oct. 2000): 208-224.

Montgomery, Gary T. "Comfort with Acculturation Status among Students from South Texas." Hispanic Journal of Behavioral Sciences. 14.2 (May 1992): 201-223.

Ortiz, Anna M. "Expressing Cultural Identity in the Learning Community: Opportunities and Challenges." New Directions for Teaching and Learning. 82 (Sum 2000): 67-79.

Oxford, Rebecca L., and Neil J. Anderson. "A Crosscultural View of Learning Styles." Language Teaching. 28.4 (Oct., 1995): 201-215.

Paredes, Americo. "The Problem of Identity in a Changing Culture: Popular Expressions of Culture Conflict Along the Lower Rio Grande Border." Borders and Identity. Ed. Smithsonian. Washington, D.C., 1996.

Perez, Samuel A. "Responding Differently to Diversity." Childhood Education. 70.3 (Spr 1994): 151-53.

Purkiss, William. "Learning Styles and the Changing Face of Community Colleges." The Importance of Learning Styles: Understanding the Implications for Learning, Course Design, and Education. Eds. Ronald R. Sims, and Serbrenia J. Sims. Westport, Connecticut: Greenwood Press, 1995. 79-98.

Reiff, Judith C. Learning Styles. Washington, D.C.: National Education Association, 1992.

Reising, R. W., and Ralph J. Hils, Jr. "Comp and Circumstance in Rural America." Freshman English News. 6.1 (Spr. 1977): 4-13.

Rivas, Maria. "Cognitive Styles of Mexican-American and Anglo-American Five, Eight, and Ten-Year Old Boys and Girls." Texas Tech Journal of Education. 11.1 (Win 1984): 67-75.

Rodrigues, Carl A., Nailin Bu, and Byung Min. "Learners' Training Approach Preference: National Culture as a Determinant." Cross Cultural Management: An International Journal. 7.1 (2000): 23-32.

Rosaldo, Renato, and William V. Flores. "Identity, conflict, and Evolving Latino Communities: Cultural Citizenship in San Jose California." Latino Cultural Citizenship: Claiming Identity, Space, and Rights. Eds. William V. Flores, and Rina Benmayor. Boston: Beacon Press, 1997. 57-96.

Salili, Farideh, Chi Yue Chiu, and Ying Yi Hong. "The Culture and Context of Learning." Farideh Salili, Chi Yue Chiu, and Ying Yi Hong, eds. Student Motivation: The Culture and Context of Learning. New York: Kluwer Academic/Plenum Publishers, 2001. 1-14.

Shaughnessy, Mina. "Some Needed Research on Writing." College Composition and Communication. 28.4 (Dec. 1977): 317-20.

Shuman, R. Baird. "Hey, Teacher, You Bloodied up My Paper!" Exercise Exchange; A Journal for Teachers of English in High Schools and Colleges. 45.2 (Spr 2000): 14-16.

Silvestrini, Blanca G. "'The World We Enter When Claiming Rights': Latinos and Their Quest for Culture." Latino Cultural Citizenship: Claiming Identity, Space, and Rights. Eds. William V. Flores, and Rina Benmayor. Boston: Beacon Press, 1997. 39-53.

Sims, Ronald R., and Serbrenia J. Sims. The Importance of Learning Styles: Understanding the Implications for Learning, Course Design, and Education. Westport, CN, 1995.

Smithsonian Institution Center for Folklife and Cultural Studies. Borders and Identity. Smithsonian Institution. Washington, D.C., 1996.

Stahl, Steven A. "Different Strokes for Different Folks? A Critique of Learning Styles." American Educator. 23.3 (Fall 1999): 27-31.

Sterling, Leroy. "Speaking and Writing, Strange Bedfellows: Some Strategies for Improving the Teaching of Writing." English in Texas. 26.3 (Spr 1995): 15-20.

Sternberg, Robert J., and Li-fang Zhang, Eds. Perspectives on Thinking Learning, and Cognitive Styles. Mahwah, NJ: Lawrence Erlbaum Associates, Publishers, 2001.

Straub, Richard. "The Student, the Text, and the Classroom Context: A Case Study of Teacher Response." Assessing Writing. 7.1 (2000): 23-55.

Swisher, Karen, and Donna Deyhle. "Styles of Learning and Learning of Styles: Educational Conflicts for American Indian/Alaskan Native Youth." Journal of Multilingual and Multicultural Development. 8.4 (1987): 345-60.

University 2000 Institutional Fact Book. Texas: The University, 2000.

Urdan, Tim. "Goal orientation and Self-Regulated Learning in the College Classroom: A Cross-Cultural Comparison." Farideh Salili, Chi Yue Chiu, and Ying Yi Hong, eds. Student Motivation: The Culture and Context of Learning. New York: Kluwer Academic/Plenum Publishers, 2001. 171-201.

Villanueva, Victor, Jr. Bootstraps: From an American Academic of Color. Urbana, IL: National Council of Teachers of English, 1993.

Volet, Simone. "Significance of Cultural and Motivational Variables on Students' Attitudes Towards Group Work." Farideh Salili, Chi Yue Chiu, and Ying Yi Hong, eds. Student Motivation: The Culture and Context of Learning. New York: Kluwer Academic/Plenum Publishers, 2001. 309-33.

Watkins, David. "Correlates of Approaches to Learning: A Cross-Cultural Meta-Analysis." Sternberg 165-195.

Witkin, Herman A. and Donald R. Goodenough. <u>Cognitive Styles: Essence and Origins: Field Dependence and Field Independence</u>. Madison, CN: International Universities Press, Inc., 1981.

Ybarra, Raul. "Latino Students and Anglo-Mainstream Instructors: A Study of Classroom Communication." <u>Journal of College Student Retention</u>. 2.2 2000-2001: 161-171.

Zhang, Li-fang. "Thinking Styles Across Cultures: Their Relationships with Student Learning." Sternberg 197-226.

INDEX

Acculturation 19
African Americans 5
Alamo 2
Amastae 4
Arevalo 1
Banks 22, 50, 60
Barnhardt 24
Battle of Alamo 2
Bilingual Chicanos 11
Bootstraps: From an American Academic of Color 24
Canabal 17, 18, 58
Canabal 51
Cantu 4
Carli, Lancia, and Paniccia 17
Cho and Forde 17, 38
Cisneros 2
Cities--Main in Counties 9
Claxton and Murrel 24, 46, 73
Clifford 78
Cities--Main in Counties 9
Davidson 12, 14, 35, 37
Dillon 14
Dreher 18
Dualistic 15, 56
Dunn, K. and Frazier 10, 35
Dunn, R. 12, 13
Elbow, Peter 80
Enculturation 19
Erickson and Erickson 10, 35
Ethnic and gender hierarchy 11
Ferguson's Law 13
Field Dependent 15, 16
Field Independent 16
Five major cultural groups 13
Florida International University in Miami 1
Freire, Paulo 93
Frisby 12-14

Gadsden Purchase 3
Garza 21, 59
Gender hierarchy 11
Generation 1.5 9
Goodenough 15, 16
Grant and Dweck 6
Griggs and R. Dunn 16, 17
Guadalupe Hidalgo Treaty 3
Guild 14, 23, 24, 25, 28, 37, 46, 48, 61, 73, 77, 80, 84, 91
Hagemann 26-28, 52, 53, 65
Harklau, Losey, and Siegal 9
Havelock 77
Hawaiians 11
Henak 14
Henderson 23, 24, 46, 61, 73
Herman Witkin 15
Hillocks 78, 79
Hispanics
  Number in University 1
  Percentage in University 1
  UT El Paso 1
Houston, Sam 2
Hudgens, B. 17
Hughes, Romeo, and Romeo 10, 47, 50, 72
Hutchinson and Beadle 22
Initiation-Response-Evaluation (IRE) 11, 30, 32, 46, 63
Inner city black youths 11
Institutional Review Board for the Protection of HumanSubjects 33, 43
IRE teaching pattern 11
Jimenez, Ricardo 15, 17, 45, 57, 58, 70, 80, 84, 85, 91
Johnson 3
Keefe and Monk 13
Khirallah 9
Killingsworth 28

Knudson 78
Kolodny 14, 38, 52
Learning task differences 12
Levy 28, 47, 48
Losey 9-11, 32, 46, 49, 51, 55, 63, 76, 84, 86, 92
Losey's "cultural mismatch theory" 56
Lower Rio Grande Valley of Texas Cities--Main in Counties 2
Counties 2
Lunsford 82
Mangan 22, 54
May 14, 1836 2
McAllen Chamber of Commerce 4
McAndrew and Hurlbert 27, 53
McDonald, Archie P. 2
McGlynn, Angela 22
Meng and Patty 91
Messick 12
Miglietti and Strange 22
Miller and Almaraz 2
Miller, Tom 3, 66, 89
Ming and Patty 16
Miville, Koonce, Darlington, and Whitlock 5, 24
Montgomery 20
Native Americans 11
Ortiz 19, 20
Ortiz and Garcia 21, 38, 51
Oxford and Anderson 21, 39, 51, 73
Pacific Islanders 13
Paredes 3
Perez 5, 22, 33, 54, 62
Perez and Banks 91
Problem 4
Purkiss 24, 26, 46, 73
Reiff 12, 37
Reising and Hils 27
Republic of the Rio Grande 3
Republic of Texas 2
Responder 74
Rio Bravo 3

Rio Grande Watershed 3
Rivas 25
Rodrigues, Bu, and Min 14
Rosaldo and Flores 18
Rural black families 11
Salili, Chiu, and Hong 5
Santa Ana 2
Schmeck 13
Shaughnessy, Mina 28
Shifting of Boundary 3
Shuman 70, 74, 75
Silenced 9
Silvestrini 18
Sims and Sims 12, 13
Smithsonian 3
Stahl 14
Sterling 26, 63, 67
Sternberg and Zhang 68
Straub 81, 82
Surnames, Spanish 4
Swisher and Deyhle 14, 5
Texas--Southern Boundary 2
Trans-Nueces Watershed 3
Treaty of Velasco 2
United States-Mexico War 3
University
First Year Composition Hispanic Ratio 1
Hispanic Ratio (total) 1
Racial Percentages 1, 2
Urdan 5
UT El Paso
Hispanic Ratio 1
Villanueva, Victor 24, 25, 39, 62, 69, 72, 92
Volet 6
Witkin 16, 91
Witkin and Goodenough 16
Working class Anglo 11
Ybarra, Raul 21, 38, 46, 49, 51, 60, 62
Zhang and Sternberg 29-31, 49, 65, 68

Appendices

Appendix A: Memo to Instructors

MEMO

To: 1301 Colleagues

From: Edye Burford

Re: Survey for dissertation research

Most of you know me, but for those of you who don't, I'll introduce myself. My name is Edith Burford, but I go by Edye. I am a Ph.D. candidate ABD which means that I have taken all of my course work and passed all of my comprehensive exams. All that I have left to complete is my dissertation. I would like you and your 1301 students to participate in a research survey. I have approval for Human Subject Research from both Indiana University of Pennsylvania (IUP) (Log No.1378) and from UTPA (Log No.87).

Appendix B: Student Informed Consent and Survey

Informed Consent Form

Dear Student:

I am a doctoral student at Indiana University of Pennsylvania (IUP) where I am conducting research for my dissertation through the IUP Graduate English Department.

The purpose of this research study is to gain insights on the teaching styles of teachers of composition courses and the learning styles of students enrolled in composition courses.

Participants in this study are asked to do the following:

1. Complete the questionnaire about your learning and teaching preferences. This will take about ten minutes.

2. Give permission to this researcher to interview you in the beginning of the semester about your preferences of classroom teaching activities which will be audio taped.

3. Give permission to this researcher to conduct a second interview later in the semester during the twelfth week regarding your preferences of classroom teaching activities which will be audio taped.

Your participation in this study is voluntary. There are no risks to you for taking part in this research. Any information obtained during this study which could identify you will be kept strictly confidential. Nowhere will you be personally identified; you will be assigned a number. Your participation will have no bearing on your academic standing or on services you received from the college or community agencies. Your questionnaire responses and your audio taped interview will be considered only in combination with that from other participants. All data collected will be kept in a collect file cabinet in my faculty office, CAS264. Upon completion of this research, all data collected during the study will be destroyed.

You may choose to participate only in the survey, part #1 above, and not in the two interviews, parts #2 and #3. Your participation in this study would be greatly appreciated. The insight gained may benefit educators by increasing their understanding of the learning styles of college students. If you are willing to participate, please sign the form below and return it along with the completed questionnaire. The form will be kept separate from your questionnaire, your interview, and any other information obtained during this study. Thank you.

Sincerely,
Edith Burford, Ph.D. Candidate
IUP Student Researcher/UTPA Lecturer
UTPA CAS 211
Edinburg, Texas 78539

Dr. Donald McAndrew
Faculty Sponsor
Graduate English Department
111 Leonard Hall
Indiana University of Pennsylvania
Indiana, PA 15705-1094

This research has been reviewed and approved by the Institutional Review Board-Human Subject's In Research. For research related problems or questions regarding subject's rights, the University of Texas Pan American (UTPA) Human Subject's Committee may be contacted through Dr. Juan Gonzalez, Chair, at 956/381-2880.
This research has been approved by the Indiana University of Pennsylvania Institutional Review Board for the Protection of Human Subjects (Phone: 724/357-2223)

I have read the information above and I consent to volunteer to participate in this study. I understand that my questionnaire responses, my interview responses, and any other information obtained during this study which could identify me are completely confidential.

NAME (PLEASE PRINT):

SIGNATURE:

WITNESS: DATE:

Student Survey

Please respond by answering the following questions on the Scantron by placing a mark next to the letter that best describes your response:
(A) Strongly agree, (B) Agree, (C) Undecided,
(D) Disagree, (E) Strongly Disagree.

1. I like it when a teacher talks or lectures about new material as a class, rather than in small groups.

2. I feel uncomfortable when the teacher tells the class to interrupt the lecture when we do not understand something or have a question.

3. I like it when the teacher asks the students to speak out in class.

4. I like it when the teacher asks the students to work on in class projects in small groups.

5. I like to try to work on projects alone, than in small groups.

6. I prefer to work alone when trying to figure out how like to do an assignment.

7. I prefer to work with others when trying to figure out how like to do an assignment.

8. I prefer a teacher with whom I can disagree and who does not get upset, but will talk out the misunderstanding with me.

9. I prefer a teacher who conducts a relaxed classroom.

10. I prefer a teacher who conducts a strictly controlled classroom.

PLEASE GIVE SHORT ANSWERS FOR THE FOLLOWING QUESTIONS

11. Which of all of your teachers did you like best? (Name not necessary, just say third grade teacher, etc.) Why did you like this teacher best?

12. Which of all of your teachers did you like least? (Name not necessary, just say third grade teacher, etc.) Why did you like this teacher Least?

13. What does a good teacher do while teaching?

14. What does a poor teacher do while teaching?

15. What does a good student do when learning new material?

16. What does a poor student do when learning new material?

17. What does an English teacher do to make an English class a good class?

18. What does an English teacher do to make an English class a boring class?

19. Do you think Hispanic teachers make good role models? Why or why not?

20. What does your family think about you attending college?

Student Survey - Page 3

I wish to participate in the interview portion of this study.

NAME								PHONE

BEST TIME TO CALL

E-MAIL ADDRESS

Appendix C: Faculty Informed Consent and Survey

Informed Consent Form

Dear Instructor:
    I am a doctoral student at Indiana University of Pennsylvania (IUP) where I am conducting research for my dissertation through the IUP Graduate English Department. The purpose of this research study is to gain insights on the teaching styles of teachers of composition courses and the learning styles of studesnts enrolled in composition courses.

Participants in this study are asked to do the following:

1. Complete the questionnaire about your learning and teaching preferences. This will take about ten minutes.
2. Give permission to this researcher to interview you in the beginning of the semester about your preferences of classroom teaching activities which will be audio taped.
3. Give permission to this researcher to conduct a second interview later in the semester during the tenth week regarding your preferences of classroom teaching activities which will be audio taped.

Your participation in this study is voluntary. There are no risks to you for taking part in this research. Any information obtained during this study which could identify you will be kept strictly confidential. Nowhere will you be personally identified; you will be assigned a number. Your participation will have no bearing on your academic standing or on services you received from the college or community agencies. Your questionnaire responses and your audio taped interview will be considered only in combination with that from other participants. All data colleted will be kept in a locked file cabinet in my faculty office, CAS264. Upon completion of this research, all data collected during the study will be destroyed.

You may choose to participate only in the survey, part #1 above, and not in the two interviews, parts #2 and #3.

Your participation in this study would be greatly appreciated. The insight gained may benefit educators by increasing their understanding of the learning styles of college students.

If you are willing to participate, please sign the form below and return it along with the completed questionnaire. The form will be kept separate from your questionnaire, your interview, and any other information obtained during this study. Thank you.

Sincerely,
Edith Burford, Ph.D. Candidate
IUP Student Researcher/UTPA Lecturer
UTPA CAS 211
Edinburg, Texas 78539

Dr. Donald McAndrew
Faculty Sponsor
Graduate English Department
111 Leonard Hall
Indiana University of Pennsylvania
Indiana, PA 15705-1094

This research has been reviewed and approved by the Institutional Review Board-Human Subject's In Research. For research related problems or questions regarding subject's rights. The University of Texas Pan American (UTPA) Human Subject's Committee may be contacted through Dr. Juan Gonzalez, Chair, at 956/381-2880.

This project has been approved by the Indiana University of Pennsylvania Institutional Review Board for the Protection of Human Subjects (Phone: 724/357-2223)

I have read the information above and I consent to volunteer to participate in this study. I understand that my questionnaire responses, my interview responses, and any other information obtained during this study which could identify me are completely confidential.

NAME (PLEASE PRINT):

SIGNATURE:

WITNESS: DATE

Faculty Survey
PLEASE GIVE SHORT ANSWERS FOR THE FOLLOWING QUESTIONS

1. Describe how do you teach writing in your classes.

2. How would you describe the students in your classes?

3. What learning problems do your students face?

4. What kind of student has been your best student?

5. What kind of student has been your worst student?

6. Do you use the work of Hispanic authors in your course? ___Yes ___No
   If you use Hispanic authors, which authors do you use?

7. Describe what you think good teaching is.

8. What are the goals for your Composition class?

9. Why do you want your students to learn to write correct English?

10. What are your hopes and aspirations for your students?

11. What do you like best about living in the Rio Grande Valley?

12. What do you like least about living in the Rio Grande Valley?

13. Do you incorporate the student's oral family history in your classes?
    ___Yes___No
    If you do, why do you do this; if you do not, why don't you do this?

14. What problems do you encounter in teaching Composition?

15. Do you like to teach Composition? ___Yes ___No

    Explain the reason for your answer.

Appendix D: Student Informed Consent and Interview

Informed Student Consent Interview Form

Dear Student:

I am a doctoral student at Indiana University of Pennsylvania (IUP) where I am conducting research for my dissertation through the IUP Graduate English Department.

The purpose of this research study is to gain insights on the teaching styles of teachers of composition courses and the learning styles of students enrolled in composition courses. Participants in this study are asked to do the following:

1. Give permission to this researcher to interview you in the beginning of the semester about your preferences of classroom teaching activities which will be audio taped. This will take about thirty minutes.
2. Give permission to this researcher to conduct a second interview later in the semester during the twelfth week regarding your preferences of classroom teaching activities which will be audio taped.

Your participation in this study is <u>voluntary</u>. You are free to decide not to participate in this study or to withdraw at any time without adversely affecting your relationship with the researcher or UTPA. There are no risks to you for taking part in this research. Any information obtained during this study which could identify you will be kept strictly confidential. Nowhere will you be personally identified; you will be assigned a number. Your participation will have no bearing on your academic standing or on services you receive from the college or community agencies. Your questionnaire responses and your audio taped interview will be considered only in combination with that from other participants. All data collected will be kept in a locked file cabinet in my faculty office, CAS264. Upon completion of this research, all data collected during the study will be destroyed.

Your participation in this study would be greatly appreciated. The insight gained may benefit educators by increasing their understanding of the learning styles of college students.

If you are willing to participate, please sign the form below and return it along with the completed questionnaire. The form will be kept separate from your questionnaire, your interview, and any other information obtained during this study. Thank you.

Sincerely,

Edith Burford, Ph.D. Candidate
IUP Student Researcher/UTPA Lecturer
UTPA CAS 211
Edinburg, Texas 78539

Dr. Donald McAndrew
Faculty Sponsor
Graduate English Department
111 Leonard Hall
Indiana University of Pennsylvania
Indiana, PA 15705-1094

This research has been reviewed and approved by the Institutional Review Board-Human Subject's In Research. For research related problems or questions regarding subject's rights, the University of Texas Pan American (UTPA) Human Subject's Committee may be contacted through Dr. Juan Gonzalez, Chair, at 956/381-2880.

This research has been approved by the Indiana University of Pennsylvania Institutional Review Board for the Protection of Human Subjects (Phone: 724/357-2223)
I have read the information above and I consent to volunteer to participate in this study. I understand that my questionnaire responses, my interview responses, and any other information obtained during this study which could identify me are completely confidential.

NAME (PLEASE PRINT)

SIGNATURE
WITNESS   DATE

PLEASE TAKE AN EXTRA UNSIGNED COPY OF THIS FORM WITH YOU.

Student Interview Questions

1. In all the English classes that you have taken, what did your favorite teacher do that you liked best?

2. In all the English classes that you have taken, what did your favorite teacher do that you liked least?

3. What teaching technique that the English teacher used helped you the most?

4. What teaching technique that the English teacher used helped you the least?

5. Do you like it when teachers put you in a group of 3 or 4 students and you read and give feedback on each other's essays?

6. What could the teacher do to encourage more class participation?

7. What do teachers do to discourage students?

8. When teachers write comments on your essays, what do you like least?

9. When teachers write comments on your essays, what do you like most?

10. Do you like it when teachers write a special note on your essays?

Appendix E: Faculty Informed Consent and Interview

Informed Consent Instructor Interview Form

Dear Instructor:

I am a doctoral student at Indiana University of Pennsylvania (IUP) where I am conducting research for my dissertation through the IUP Graduate English Department.

The purpose of this research study is to gain insights on the teaching styles of teachers of composition courses and the learning styles of students enrolled in composition courses.

Participants in this study are asked to:

1. Give permission to this researcher to interview you in the beginning of the semester about your preferences of classroom teaching activities which will be audio taped. This will take about thirty minutes.

2. Give permission to this researcher to conduct a second interview later in the semester during the tenth week regarding your preferences of classroom teaching activities which will be audio taped.

Your participation in this study is voluntary. You are free to decide not to participate in this study or to withdraw at any time without adversely affecting your relationship with the researcher. There are no risks to you for taking part in this research. Any information obtained during this study which could identify you will be kept strictly confidential. Nowhere will you be personally identified; you will be assigned a number. Your participation will have no bearing on your professional standing with the university. Your questionnaire responses and your audio taped interview will be considered only in combination with that from other participants. All data colleted will be kept in a locked file cabinet in my faculty office, CAS264. Upon completion of this research, all data collected during the study will be destroyed.

Your participation in this study would be greatly appreciated. The insight gained may benefit educators by increasing their understanding of the teaching styles of First-Year Composition teachers and the learning styles of college students.

If you are willing to participate, please sign the form below and return it along with the completed questionnaire. The form will be kept separate from your questionnaire, your interview, and any other information obtained during this study. Thank you.

Sincerely,

Edith Burford, Ph.D. Candidate
IUP Student Researcher/UTPA Lecturer
UTPA CAS 211
Edinburg, Texas 78539

Dr. Donald McAndrew
Faculty Sponsor
Graduate English Department
111 Leonard Hall
Indiana University of Pennsylvania
Indiana, PA 15705-1094

This research has been reviewed and approved by the Institutional Review Board-Human Subject's In Research. For research related problems or questions regarding subject's rights, The

University of Texas Pan American (UTPA) Human Subject's Committee may be contacted through Dr. Juan Gonzalez, Chair, at 956/381-2880.
<u>This project has been approved by the Indiana University of Pennsylvania Institutional Review Board for the Protection of Human Subjects (Phone: 724/357-2223)</u>

I have read the information above and I consent to volunteer to participate in this study. I understand that my questionnaire responses and any other information obtained during this study which could identify me are completely confidential.

NAME (PLEASE PRINT)

SIGNATURE

WITNESS   DATE

PLEASE TAKE AN EXTRA UNSIGNED COPY OF THIS FORM WITH YOU.

Instructor Interview Questions

1. How do you explain what an essay is to students?

2. How do you explain the process of writing to students?

3. What do you look for in student writing?

4. What do you consider good writing?

5. How do you deal with students who have difficulty in grasping academic writing?

6. How do you encourage class participation?

7. Do you group students to read each other's essays and give feedback? Why or why not?

8. When grading essays, what errors do you mark?

9. Do you write end notes on essays? Why or why not?

10. If you write notes, what do you write in them?

Appendix F: Map of Texas Showing Counties

TEXAS - Counties

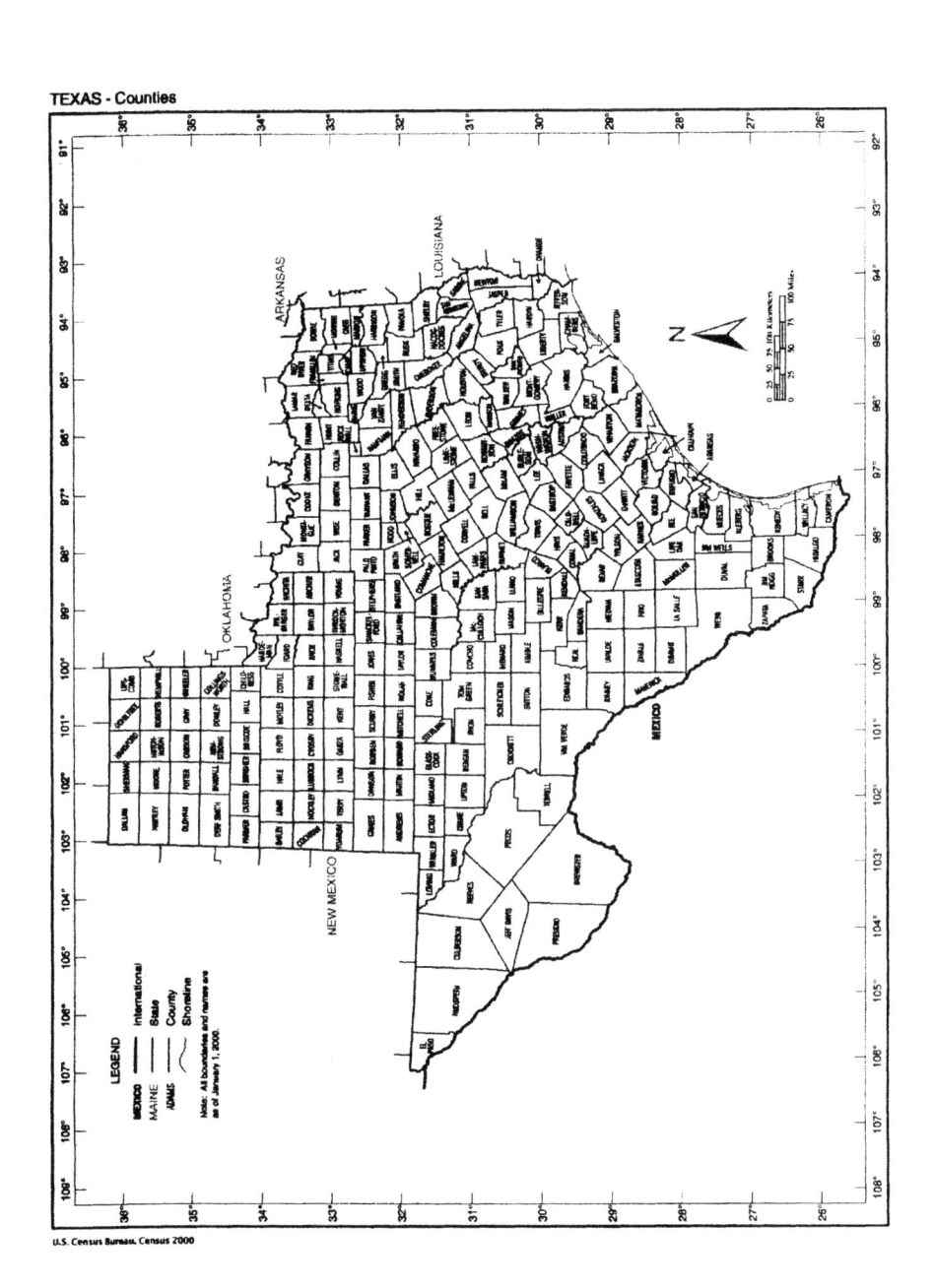

TEXAS
www.50states.com

MELLEN STUDIES IN EDUCATION

1. C. J. Schott, **Improving The Training and Evaluation of Teachers at the Secondary School Level: Educating the Educators in Pursuit of Excellence**
2. Manfred Prokop, **Learning Strategies For Second Language Users: An Analytical Appraisal with Case Studies**
3. Charles P. Nemeth, **A Status Report on Contemporary Criminal Justice Education: A Definition of the Discipline and an Assessment of Its Curricula, Faculty and Program Characteristics**
4. Stephen H. Barnes (ed.), **Points of View on American Higher Education: A Selection of Essays from** *The Chronicle of Higher Education* (Volume 1) **Professors and Scholarship**
5. Stephen H. Barnes (ed.), **Points of View on American Higher Education: A Selection of Essays from** *The Chronicle of Higher Education* (Volume 2) **Institutions and Issues**
6. Stephen H. Barnes (ed.), **Points of View on American Higher Education: A Selection of Essays from** *The Chronicle of Higher Education* (Volume 3) **Students and Standards**
7. Michael V. Belok and Thomas Metos, **The University President in Arizona 1945-1980: An Oral History**
8. Henry R. Weinstock and Charles J. Fazzaro, **Democratic Ideals and the Valuing of Knowledge In American Education: Two Contradictory Tendencies**
9. Arthur R. Crowell, Jr., **A Handbook For the Special Education Administrator: Organization and Procedures for Special Education**
10. J.J. Chambliss, **The Influence of Plato and Aristotle on John Dewey's Philosophy**
11. Alan H. Levy, **Elite Education and the Private School: Excellence and Arrogance at Phillips Exeter Academy**
12. James J. Van Patten (ed.), **Problems and Issues in College Teaching and Higher Education Leadership**
13. Célestin Freinet, **The Wisdom of Matthew: An Essay in Contemporary French Educational Theory**, John Sivell (trans.)
14. Francis R. Phillips, **Bishop Beck and English Education, 1949-1959**
15. Gerhard Falk, **The Life of the Academic Professional in America: An Inventory of Tasks, Tensions & Achievements**
16. Phillip Santa Maria, **The Question of Elementary Education in the Third Russian State Duma, 1907-1912**
17. James J. Van Patten (ed.), **The Socio-Cultural Foundations of Education and the Evolution of Education Policies in the U.S.**
18. Peter P. DeBoer, **Origins of Teacher Education at Calvin Colege, 1900-1930: And Gladly Teach**
19. Célestin Freinet, **Education Through Work: A Model for Child-Centered Learning**, John Sivell (trans.)
20. John Sivell (ed.), **Freinet Pedagogy: Theory and Practice**
21. John Klapper, **Foreign-Language Learning Through Immersion**

22. Maurice Whitehead, **The Academies of the Reverend Bartholomew Booth in Georgian England and Revolutionary America**
23. Margaret D. Tannenbaum, **Concepts and Issues in School Choice**
24. Rose M. Duhon-Sells and Emma T. Pitts, **An Interdisciplinary Approach to Multicultural Teaching and Learning**
25. Robert E. Ward, **An Encyclopedia of Irish Schools, 1500-1800**
26. David A. Brodie, **A Reference Manual for Human Performance Measurement in the Field of Physical Education and Sports Sciences**
27. Xiufeng Liu, **Mathematics and Science Curriculum Change in the People's Republic of China**
28. Judith Evans Longacre, **The History of Wilson College 1868 to 1970**
29. Thomas E. Jordan, **The First Decade of Life, Volume I: Birth to Age Five**
30. Thomas E. Jordan, **The First Decade of Life, Volume II: The Child From Five to Ten Years**
31. Mary I. Fuller and Anthony J. Rosie (eds.), **Teacher Education and School Partnerships**
32. James J. Van Patten (ed.), **Watersheds in Higher Education**
33. K. (Moti) Gokulsing and Cornel DaCosta (eds.), **Usable Knowledges as the Goal of University Education: Innovations in the Academic Enterprise Culture**
34. Georges Duquette (ed.), **Classroom Methods and Strategies for Teaching at the Secondary Level**
35. Linda A. Jackson and Michael Murray, **What Students Really Think of Professors: An Analysis of Classroom Evaluation Forms at an American University**
36. Donald H. Parkerson and Jo Ann Parkerson, **The Emergence of the Common School in the U.S. Countryside**
37. Neil R. Fenske, **A History of American Public High Schools, 1890-1990: Through the Eyes of Principals**
38. Gwendolyn M. Duhon Boudreaux (ed.), **An Interdisciplinary Approach to Issues and Practices in Teacher Education**
39. John Roach, **A Regional Study of Yorkshire Schools 1500-1820**
40. V.J. Thacker, **Using Co-operative Inquiry to Raise Awareness of the Leadership and Organizational Culture in an English Primary School**
41. Elizabeth Monk-Turner, **Community College Education and Its Impact on Socioeconomic Status Attainment**
42. George A. Churukian and Corey R. Lock (eds.), **International Narratives on Becoming a Teacher Educator: Pathways to a Profession**
43. Cecilia G. Manrique and Gabriel G. Manrique, **The Multicultural or Immigrant Faculty in American Society**
44. James J. Van Patten (ed.), **Challenges and Opportunities for Education in the 21st Century**
45. Barry W. Birnbaum, **Connecting Special Education and Technology for the 21st Century**

46. J. David Knottnerus and Frédérique Van de Poel-Knottnerus, **The Social Worlds of Male and Female Children in the Nineteenth Century French Educational System: Youth, Rituals, and Elites**
47. Sandra Frey Stegman, **Student Teaching in the Choral Classroom: An Investigation of Secondary Choral Music Student Teachers' Perceptions of Instructional Successes and Problems as They Reflect on Their Music Teaching**
48. Gwendolyn M. Duhon and Tony Manson (eds.), **Preparation, Collaboration, and Emphasis on the Family in School Counseling for the New Millennium**
49. Katherina Danko-McGhee, **The Aesthetic Preferences of Young Children**
50. Jane Davis-Seaver, **Critical Thinking in Young Children**
51. Gwendolyn M. Duhon and Tony J. Manson (eds.), **Implications for Teacher Education – Cross-Ethnic and Cross-Racial Dynamics of Instruction**
52. Samuel Mitchell, **Partnerships in Creative Activities Among Schools, Artists and Professional Organizations Promoting Arts Education**
53. Loretta Niebur, **Incorporating Assessment and the National Standards for Music Education into Everyday Teaching**
54. Tony Del Valle, **Written Literacy Features of Three Puerto Rican Family Networks in Chicago: An Ethnographic Study**
55. Christine J. Villani and Colin C. Ward, **Violence and Non-Violence in the Schools: A Manual for Administration**
56. Michael Dallaire, **Contemplation in Liberation – A Method for Spiritual Education in the Schools**
57. Gwendolyn M. Duhon, **Problems and Solutions in Urban Schools**
58. Paul Grosch, **Recognition of the Spirit and Its Development as Legitimate Concerns of Education**
59. D. Antonio Cantu, **An Investigation of the Relationship Between Social Studies Teachers' Beliefs and Practice**
60. Loretta Walton Jaggers, Nanthalia W. McJamerson and Gwendolyn M. Duhon (eds.), **Developing Literacy Skills Across the Curriculum: Practical, Approaches, Creative Models, Strategies, and Resources**
61. Haim Gordon and Rivca Gordon, **Sartre's Philosophy and the Challenge of Education**
62. Robert D. Buchanan and Ruth Ann Roberts, **Performance-Based Evaluation for Certificated and Non-Certificated School Personnel: Standards, Criteria, Indicators, Models**
63. C. David Warner III, **Opinions of Administrators, Faculty, and Students Regarding Academic Freedom and Student Artistic Expression**
64. Robert D. Heslep, **A Philosophical Guide for Decision Making by Educators: Developing a Set of Foundational Principles**
65. Noel P. Hurley, **How You Speak Determines How You Learn: Resource Allocation and Student Achievement**
66. Barry W. Birnbaum, **Foundations and Practices in the Use of Distance Education**

67. Franklin H. Silverman and Robert Moulton, **The Impact of a Unique Cooperative American University USAID Funded Speech-Language Pathologist, Audiologist, and Deaf Educator B.S. Degree Program in the Gaza Strip**
68. Tony J. Manson (ed.), **Teacher Education Preparation for Diversity**
69. Scott D. Robinson, **Autobiostories Promoting Emotional Insights into the Teaching and Learning of Secondary Science**
70. Francis Oakley, **The Leadership Challenge of a College Presidency: Meaning, Occasion, and Voice**
71. Melvin D. Williams, **The Ethnography of an Anthropology Department, 1959-1979: An Academic Village**
72. Kevin McGuinness, **The Concept of Academic Freedom**
73. Alastair Sharp, **Reading Comprehension and Text Organization**
74. Nicholas Beattie, **The Freinet Movements of France, Italy, and Germany, 1920-2000: Versions of Educational Progressivism**
75. Anne P. Chapman, **Language Practices in School Mathematics: A Social Semiotic Approach**
76. Wendy Robinson, **Pupil Teachers and Their Professional Training in Pupil-Teacher Centres in England and Wales, 1870-1914**
77. Barbara A. Sposet, **The Affective and Cognitive Development of Culture Learning During the Early and Middle Childhood Curriculum**
78. John P. Anchan and Shiva S. Halli, **Exploring the Role of the Internet in Global Education**
79. James J. Van Patten and Timothy J. Bergen, **A Case Study Approach to a Multi-Cultural Mosaic in Education**
80. Jeffrey L. Hoogeveen, **The Role of Students in the History of Composition**
81. Rose M. Duhon-Sells and Leslie Agard-Jones (eds.), **Educators Leading the Challenge to Alleviate School Violence**
82. Rose Marie Duhon-Sells, Halloway C. Sells, Alice Duhon-Ross, Gwendolyn Duhon, Glendolyn Duhon-JeanLouis (eds.) **International Perspectives on Methods of Improving Education Focusing on the Quality of Diversity**
83. Ruth Rees, **A New Era in Educational Leadership–One Principal, Two Schools: Twinning**
84. Daniel J. Mahoney, **An Organizational, Social-Psychological, and Ethical Analysis of School Administrators' Use of Deception**
85. Judith Longacre, **The Trial and Renewal of Wilson College**
86. Michael Delucchi, **Student Satisfaction with Higher Education During the 1970s—A Decade of Social Change**
87. Samuel Mitchell, **The Value of Educational Partnerships Worldwide with the Arts, Science, Business, and Community Organizations**
88. Susan Davis Lenski and Wendy L. Black (eds.), **Transforming Teacher Education Through Partnerships**
89. Ana Maria Klein, **Learning How Children Process Mathematical Problems**
90. Laura Shea Doolan, **The History of the International Learning Styles Network and Its Impact on Educational Innovation**

91. Gail Singleton Taylor (ed.), **The Impact of High-Stakes Testing on the Academic Futures of Non-Mainstream Students**
92. G.R. Evans, **Inside the University of Cambridge in the Modern World**
93. Agnes D. Walkinshaw, **Integrating Drama with Primary and Junior Education: The Ongoing Debate**
94. Joe Marshall Hardin and Ray Wallace (eds.), **Teaching, Research, and Service in the Twenty-First Century English Department: A Delicate Balance**
95. Samuel Mitchell, Patricia Klinck, and John Burger (eds.), **Worldwide Partnerships for Schools with Voluntary Organizations, Foundations, Universities, Companies, and Community Councils**
96. Emerson D. Case, **Making the Transition from an Intensive English Program to Mainstream University Courses–An Ethnographic Study**
97. Roberta A. McKay and Susan E. Gibson, **Social Studies for the 21st Century–A Review of Current Literature and Research**
98. Edith Sue Kohner Burford, **Investigating the Reasons University Students in the South Central United States Have to Retake First-Year English Composition**
99. Christina Isabelli-García, **A Case Study of the Factors in the Development of Spanish Linguistic Accuracy and Oral Communication Skills: Motivation and Extended Interaction in the Study Abroad Context**
100. Rose Duhon-Sells (ed.), **Best Practices for Teaching Students in Urban Schools**
101. Wendy P. Hope, **The Impact of Teachers' Perceptions and Pedagogical Practices on the Educational Experiences of Immigrant Students from the Commonwealth Caribbean**
102. Mary Catherine Daly, **Developing the Whole Child–The Importance of the Emotional, Social, Moral, and Spiritual in Early Years Education and Care**